Attacking the
Standardized Exam

Attacking the Standardized Exam

The Art of Mastering Multiple Choice Standardized Tests

RONALD S. THOMPSON
MBA, JD, CCIM, CRE, CLU, ChFC, CFP, NREMT-P

Former
Captain, US Marine Corps, and
Assistant Dean of the University of Detroit Law School

authorHOUSE®

AuthorHouse™
1663 Liberty Drive
Bloomington, IN 47403
www.authorhouse.com
Phone: 1-800-839-8640

First published by AuthorHouse   11/04/2011

ISBN: 978-1-4634-2207-3 (sc)
ISBN: 978-1-4634-2206-6 (hc)
ISBN: 978-1-4634-2205-9 (ebk)

Library of Congress Control Number: 2011910573

Printed in the United States of America

This Book Will:

- Boost Your Confidence

- Eliminate "Test Stress"

- Focus Your Study Time

- Fully Prepare You For Test Day

- Give You Proven Systems For Success

- Teach You To "Guess" Correctly

- Significantly Improve Your Score

This book and all my life's work is dedicated to Susan K. Thompson, my greatest inspiration, best friend, soul mate, mother of my children, and loving wife of nearly thirty-two years. The thousands of tests I have taken to allow me to write this book—and for that matter, everything that I have done that has been worthwhile—has been a direct result of her love, support, and motivation throughout the years.

About the Author

Ronald S. Thompson is an estate, business, and tax planning attorney; financial planner; and real estate consultant. He currently holds the following degrees, licenses, and certifications: bachelor of general studies, University of Michigan; master of business administration, Boston University; Juris Doctor, University of Detroit School of Law; licensed attorney in Michigan and Ohio; licensed residential builder; licensed real estate broker; series 7, 63, and 65 securities register investment advisor; licensed health, life, property, and casualty insurance producer; national registry emergency medical technician/ paramedic; certified commercial investment member (CCIM); counselor of real estate (CRE); chartered life underwriter (CLU); chartered financial consultant (ChFC); and certified financial planner (CFP).

In achieving the foregoing degrees, licenses, and certifications, Ron has taken, "mastered," and passed more than one thousand multiple-choice exams. He has also taken dozens of professional test preparation courses. Ron's background also includes service as a commissioned officer in the United States Marine Corps and as assistant dean at the University of Detroit School of Law. Ron uses the sum total of all of the knowledge and experienced he has gained through both formal education and life experience to teach both innovative and commonsense approaches to taking and "mastering" multiple-choice exams.

Introduction

I have spent the better part of the past fifty-three years taking well over a thousand multiple-choice tests. As a teenager, I struggled through high school. Armed with an average IQ and some fairly significant learning disabilities, I barely graduated with a 1.4 grade point average. However, I was smart enough to figure out early on that achieving success in academics had far more to do with the ability to master multiple-choice tests than raw intellect. From there, I began a thirty-five-year study on the art and science of passing, mastering, and scoring high on multiple-choice tests.

Despite a very substandard high school GPA, I scored high enough on the SAT and the ACT to be accepted to the University of Michigan, one of the top academic institutions in the country. Upon graduation from college, I accepted a commission as an officer in the United States Marine Corps. As a US Marine officer, I completed dozens of military and civilian schools, including a master's degree from Boston University and a Juris Doctor degree from the University of Detroit School of Law. In fact, I earned a full-ride military scholarship to law school based primarily on the fact that I scored so highly on the law school aptitude test (ninety-eighth percentile). Upon completion of law school, I passed the Michigan bar exam on the first attempt, scoring 149 points on the multistate (the multiple-choice portion of the exam), which was one question away from automatic passage (at 150, the examiners do not need to grade the essay portion). I have also taken and applied many of the Marine Corps concepts of discipline and mental toughness to the art of preparing for, taking, and passing multiple-choice tests.

Resigning my commission and leaving the Marine Corps in 1990, I continued both my education as well as my quest to hone my test-taking skills. I currently hold twelve professional licenses and five professional designations, which required me to pass several comprehensive and difficult multiple-choice examinations. I have also attended dozens of professional test preparation courses. From those courses, I have cherry-picked all of the valuable lessons and test-taking tips and have included those in this book.

One of the professional licenses I hold is a paramedic license. As a paramedic, I have gained a much greater understanding of the anatomy and physiology of test taking. Test taking is all about the central nervous system, which, of course, includes the brain. However, as I explain in this book, it is clear that the sympathetic and parasympathetic nervous systems have as much to do with passing and failing multiple-choice tests as the brain. Accordingly, I have also applied many of those principles in this book.

The purpose and intent of this book is to provide the reader with all of the tools and weapons necessary to attack, conquer, and ultimately master multiple-choice exams. Through reading this book, you will achieve the following skills:

1. Develop the mental toughness to achieve total test-taking confidence
2. Eliminate fear, stress, test anxiety, and other psychological barriers to test success
3. Achieve the discipline and decisiveness necessary to prepare for, attack, and conquer the exam
4. Build the "test mastering body" through proper exercise, diet, and sleeping habits
5. Learn focused memorization techniques designed to limit study time and achieve superior results
6. Understand the test preparation methodologies that actually work and how to select the best one for you, including study courses, sample tests, and flash cards

7. Build a comprehensive and stress-free study schedule for guaranteed success
8. Learn how to focus on what you actually need to know to pass the exam and how to best prepare to retrieve that information at test time
9. Understand why the last twenty-four hours before the exam are so critical and learn a step-by-step program of exactly how to use that time to maximize your test results
10. Know what to eat before the exam, what to wear and bring to the exam, and the critical steps to accomplish upon arrival at the test site
11. Understand how to attack questions and the correct system to locate and select the right answer every time, all while properly managing your time to ensure no questions go unanswered
12. Develop the skills required to win the "game" of test taking, including the rules of logic and statistics that will lead you to the right answer and show you how, when necessary, to guess logically and intelligently, significantly increasing your odds of success

Over the years, I have helped many individuals study for and pass multiple-choice examinations. My hope is that with this book, I can help even more.

Chapter 1

Developing "Mental Toughness" to Attack and Beat the Exam

Step One: Building the Biological Foundation

A. Preparation is key.

As a Boy Scout, the most important lesson I learned was based on the Boy Scout motto "be prepared." Clearly, the success of facing any challenge is based 99 percent on preparedness (I will give 1 percent to luck and no more). After twelve years as a Marine Corps officer, I realized nothing could be truer than that concept. However, being prepared usually means much more than merely studying the challenge or studying for the challenge. If you want to meet the challenge, you must *ready yourself* for the challenge, not only intellectually but emotionally and physically. By being ready for the challenge on all three levels—physical, emotional, and intellectual—you will not only meet the challenge, but you will master it. Nothing could be truer when preparing for a multiple-choice exam. So let's begin by looking at developing physical and emotional toughness.

B. Mental toughness starts with physical toughness, and physical toughness starts with fitness.

As previously stated, maximizing your performance on a multiple-choice exam requires preparedness. There are three aspects of being prepared: physical preparation, emotional preparation, and intellectual preparation. In order to be truly intellectually prepared, you need to have the right attitude, which requires emotional preparation. In order to be emotionally prepared, you must have the right physical preparation. While all three aspects are covered in detail in this book, we will start with physical preparation as it is the foundation for the other two.

The Marine Corps teaches you mental toughness. Early on in boot camp, young US Marines are trained to understand (*not* believe but *understand*) that nothing is impossible. If you set out to accomplish the mission and are ready to do whatever it takes to accomplish the mission, then the mission can be accomplish—*period*! That aspect of psychology, as it applies to test taking, will be dealt with in some detail later in the book.

However, the Marine Corps also trains you to be prepared for the task, and that requires not only intellectual readiness but also physical readiness. That is why the Marine Corps, far more than any other military service organization, prides itself on developing and maintaining the physical fitness of its members across the board. When you are in good physical shape, you are in better mental shape. You can study longer, absorb more information, and stay focused for greater periods of time. You are also less prone to stress and less affected by it. In addition, physical exercise can reduce and/or relieve stress.

Going back to paramedic training, productive brain activity has a great deal to do with flow of oxygen to the brain. Oxygen is carried to the brain and other organs through hemoglobin contained in the blood. Interestingly, an overweight person will typically have less blood volume that a person of normal weight who is the same height. Likewise, an athlete will typically have greater blood volume than a nonathlete of the same height and weight. So the better physical condition you are in, the better your blood capacity and the greater opportunity for oxygen flow to the brain. So the first step toward preparation for taking and mastering a multiple-choice test is to get into shape.

Of course, I am not suggesting that you need to train for and run a marathon. However, the point here is to begin a regular regiment of exercise and good diet. While later in the book I discuss specific foods you should and should not eat immediately prior to and during a multiple-choice examination, here I am simply talking about the concept of eating right. Regarding exercise, specifics of that are also very individual and beyond the scope of this chapter or book.

However, there is another important point to be made here. When studying for a very important multiple-choice examination (ACT, LSAT, MEDCAT, bar examination, CFP, etc.), it is not uncommon for people to work out less or stop working out completely in order to focus more time on studying. Nothing could be worse that that. In fact, regular exercise promotes better sleeping habits and rest, which ultimately allows you to sleep sounder for fewer hours and focus better while awake. So make sure you get in shape and stay in shape. Once you are in good physical shape, you are ready to begin the second and third aspects of good test preparation, which are emotional preparation and intellectual preparation.

C. The physiology of test taking: avoid triggering the sympathetic nervous system.

As a paramedic, you learn a great deal about human anatomy and physiology. While heart, lungs, and kidneys serve critical functions, it is the central nervous system that ultimately controls the body.

Of course, the major component of the central nervous system is the brain. Most people believe that it is the brain that is the sole determiner of whether you pass or fail a test, but the truth is that's only one aspect. The other aspects, which are very critical, are two subsystems of the autonomic nervous system known as the sympathetic and parasympathetic nervous systems. The best way to describe these two systems is to refer to them as they are commonly known. The sympathetic nervous system is known as the fight or flight system, or the accelerator. The parasympathetic nervous system is known as the feed and breed system, or the brakes.

When a person is placed in a stressful situation, the sympathetic nervous system kicks in. Noradrenalin is secreted, and the body reacts. Pupils dilate, and heart rate and blood pressure increase. Blood flow begins diverting to the muscles and lungs in anticipation of fight (self-defense through physical force) or flight (running away from danger). When this reaction is prolonged, adrenalin is secreted, increasing the reaction. Sweating and vomiting typically occur. After this event, the body is exhausted, resulting in a crash similar to that described in many energy drink commercials.

For the foregoing reasons, constant triggering of the sympathetic nervous system through needless worrying over time creates physical and mental exhaustion. Of course, none of this is good for a person preparing for a test. A good test taker wants to maintain a parasympathetic system. Here, blood flows to the stomach, encouraging good digestion and nutrient absorption. Better yet, all of the stress-producing aspects of the sympathetic nervous system are absent. So the first goal in developing physical toughness is eliminating worry and stress.

Obviously, thorough intellectual preparation for a test will build confidence and, therefore, reduce stress, which we will get to later. However, let's begin by looking at reducing worry and stress through physical strength.

D. The physiology of test taking: foods that help you pass tests and foods that cause you to fail.

It is no secret that nutrition plays a critical role in learning. Hence, top performance in test taking requires more than just eating right in general. More specifically, it requires you to consume the right foods prior to and, when applicable, during the test.

As stated previously, chemicals produced by the human body have tremendous effects on both our psychology and physiology. Specifically, when the body produces norepinephrine and dopamine, the brain is stimulated, and your ability to think and reason is enhanced. Conversely, production of serotonin acts as a calming mechanism on the brain, which, in fact, creates fatigue and decreased ability to think and reason. Additionally, eating foods that cause quick energy surges typically result in a resulting fatigue or a crash. Put another way, when you have energy and are alert, you are a better test taker. When you are fatigued and sleepy, you are a poor test taker.

Foods containing protein and protein mixed with carbohydrates enhance production of norepinephrine and dopamine, so these foods should be consumed before taking a test. If you are testing in the morning, eat a healthy breakfast consisting of one or more of the following: eggs, lean meat, whole grain toast, high fiber whole grain cereal (without sugar and with skim or low-fat milk), yogurt, and fruit. Avoid quick energy foods, such as sugary cereals, fatty meats (like bacon), energy drinks, and large amounts of coffee.

If you are testing in the afternoon, eat a healthy breakfast and a healthy lunch consisting of peanut butter (no jelly) or a lean meat sandwich on whole grain bread, fruit, and yogurt. Again, avoid fatty or sugary foods and quick energy foods and drinks. Also, you should avoid foods that contain the amino acid tryptophan, which is contained in turkey, milk, corn, beans, and brown rice. This amino acid causes the production of niacin, which in turn causes the production of serotonin. Alcohol consumption should also be avoided prior to taking an exam for all the obvious reasons.

Now that you have learned how to properly build the physical test-taking machine, we will next discuss the development of psychological toughness.

Chapter 2

Developing "Mental Toughness" to Attack and Beat the Exam

Step Two: Building the Psychological Foundation

A. The Psychology of not "Taking" but "Beating" the Exam.

The Marine Corps trains you to be tough, but you learn early on that mental toughness is actually far more important than physical toughness. I remember the first time I really took a close look at the US Marines who had been awarded the Congressional Medal of Honor. My expectation was that these individuals would have all been champion athletes and street fighters. I was surprised to learn that, in fact, the majority of those guys were just regular people who shared one exceptional set of abilities. When confronted with a very difficult and stressful situation, they were able to focus, be decisive and disciplined, and then use those very skills to accomplish the impossible.

Focus, discipline, and decisiveness are *not* inbred. They are *learned* traits and skill sets. They are also the very same skill sets that help you properly study for, take, and pass multiple-choice exams. The intent of this book is to help you embrace the concepts and develop those skills. If you truly believe you will pass the exam and you have properly prepared for the exam (which means far more than just studying for it), you *will* pass the exam.

B. Developing Confidence.

Confidence is the single most important requirement when facing *any* challenge. It is also, in my view, the single most important prerequisite to passing a multiple-choice test. If you sit for an exam and lack confidence in your ability to pass that exam, you will not pass it. You can study and learn the material at a level that would allow you to teach it to others, but if you lack confidence, you will not pass the exam, plain and simple.

When you are not confident in your ability to pass an exam, several things will automatically happen that will significantly reduce your likelihood of success. First, because you lack confidence, you will be nervous and worried both prior to and during the exam. As discussed earlier, the sympathetic nervous system kicks in, and your body and brain are working against you. When preparing for an exam, you need to be focused. Worry, concern, stress, and other by-products of lack of confidence will kill your focus and significantly hurt your ability to pass the test.

Second, while taking the test, lack of confidence can be disastrous. Not only because of the physiological concerns previously discussed but also because it results in self-doubt and indecisiveness. Instead of methodically and systematically going about the task of attacking and answering the questions, you will nervously read each question with lack of focus and then question and second guess yourself when selecting answers later. You may also go back and change answers out of self-doubt, and, if the exam is more than a few minutes long, you will grow physically and mentally exhausted in the process.

In the end, you will fail. After that first failure, your confidence will suffer even more, and the second time around with that test is not likely to go any better. So you must become confident. That is the absolute first and most important requirement for building mental toughness in preparation for a test.

During World War II, the Marine Corps was engaged in what is often termed the island-hopping campaign. This was essentially the systematic attacking and seizing of several strategic Japanese islands containing military strongholds. One of those islands was Tarawa. Tarawa was an island that was really nothing more than the top of a volcano sticking out of the Pacific. It was made up of solid volcanic rock and housed thousands of Japanese fighting positions dug deep into the rock going up a steep uphill grade. Inside those fighting positions were thousands of Japanese soldiers armed with machine guns and mortars, all of whom were ready to fight to the death, without exception.

When US Army strategists studied the Island, they concluded that it could *not* be taken (using their terms) "by a million men in a million years." Despite that expert opinion, the Marine Corps took Tarawa with a single reinforced US Marine division in seventy-six hours! They accomplished the impossible. By all standards, it *was* impossible. However, the taking of Tarawa was made possible by preparation and training, but above all, it was made possible by *confidence*. When the Marines landed, they were confident. Truth be told, they were likely scared out of their minds for very good reason, but they were confident in their ability to accomplish the mission, and they did, plain and simple.

When taking a multiple-choice test, you need to approach it the same way. You should not take the test; you should attack the test. So how do we gain confidence in addition to preparing for the test through studying the material to be tested? We begin by eliminating fear.

C. Eliminating Fear.

Fear is a very devastating emotion. Fear is frequently irrational and *always* detrimental to accomplishing the mission. To really eliminate fear, one must understand it. Fear is a reaction to the perception of danger. It is a self-preservation mechanism inherent in all creatures, both highly developed ones like humans and far less developed ones like insects.

When fear is triggered in humans, the sympathetic nervous system kicks in as previously discussed. If danger truly exists, the resulting physical reactions are certainly a plus. But when preparing for and taking a test, they are useless, counterproductive, and occasionally devastating. In addition to robbing valuable blood and oxygen flow from the brain, where you most need it, the eventual ceasing of the adrenaline flow creates a crash and then exhaustion.

So if we have established that fear is bad, then how do we eliminate it? The first step is to analyze and rationalize the reason for the fear. In the case of a multiple-choice test, the fear is almost always irrational.

For example, if failed or poorly performed on, the vast majority of multiple-choice tests can simply be retaken. Many others are less significant in and of themselves, as they may be weighed against other tests or other nontesting factors. For example, academic aptitude tests, such as the ACT, SAT, GRE, GMAT, and LSAT, are also heavily counterbalanced by grade point average and/or other factors. Multiple-choice tests can also frequently be retaken with a combined score average. So typically fear in advance of or during an exam is irrational and illogical and should be eliminated. Let's begin by analyzing the psychology of fear.

All three of my sons were high school wrestlers. My oldest son, Ronnie Thompson, started wrestling as a high school freshman. Weighing about eighty pounds and having zero experience, he began his wrestling career as a perpetual nervous wreck. I remember watching him pace nervously back and forth on the mat prior to every match. While other kids were busy stretching and warming up for their matches, Ronnie was biting his nails and worrying. When it came time to wrestle, he was already exhausted and had mentally lost the match before the first whistle blew.

Between his junior and senior year, he attended a very well known wrestling camp at the University of Minnesota known as J. Robinson. There he learned confidence and mental toughness. Much like Marine Corps boot camp, he was taught to go into every match assuming he would win. The concept was to not ask who your opponent was or even care who your opponent was, just know you will win and go wrestle the match you were trained to wrestle. If you lose, leave it on the mat, figure out what you can do better next time, and go about the task of preparing to win the next match.

When Ronnie entered his senior season, he never paced again. He went into every match confident and never spent one minute worrying. He wrestled his way to the state championship match that year and went on to become an outstanding Division I college wrestler. The point of the story is simply this: once you conquer you own fears, nothing can stop you. So the first requirement of multiple-choice test preparation is gaining confidence by eliminating fear. Of course, telling someone to not be afraid is easy. Getting them to not be afraid is a bit more difficult, so let's talk about the intellectual side of eliminating fear.

D. Embracing Determinism.

When I was in college, I was a nervous wreck. Attending the University of Michigan, I soon realized I was significantly outmatched intellectually by most of my fellow students. Most of my classmates were brainiacs, while I was just a dumb kid who knew how to take multiple-choice tests.

An additional fear factor was the fact that most of my classes were graded on a curve. That meant that a B was not between 80 and 90 percent (as is typically the case). Instead, you received a B if your score was in the top 10 to 20 percent of the class scores. In essence, I was significantly outmanned and outgunned. Soon I began burning holes in the lining of my stomach with worry and stress, to a point where I became physically ill.

Then I had the opportunity to take a philosophy class that forever changed my life. In that class, we learned about many of the great intellectual debates. One of those classic debates was free will vs. determinism. The philosophy of free will basically suggests that every individual makes free choices that determine his own destiny. The concept of determinism, on the other hand, embraces the idea that man has no free will and that everything is predestined. In the simplest of terms, when someone is born, he simply goes through life experiencing and reacting to events in a programmed way and eventually dies at the predesignated time.

This particular debate intrigued me, and I eventually came to conclude that the concept of determinism had merit. After all, I think most people will acknowledge that when confronted with a "choice," people will tend to make certain predictable choices based on their upbringing, personality, and needs at the time. Likewise, I do not think that many people, even those who completely embrace the concept of free will, would debate that certain events are unavoidable.

So then what does this have to do with preparing for and taking a multiple-choice exam? Simply this: understand that the test you will be handed is the test you will be handed. There is nothing you can do, at least not legitimately, to change that. The questions on the exam will be the ones on the exam. Again, that is a piece of destiny you cannot alter. So ultimately, worrying about an exam before, during, or after you take it serves absolutely no legitimate purpose.

Finally, and perhaps most importantly, you will either be prepared to answer the questions correctly and pass the test, or you won't, plain and simple. So then, what possible purpose does worry and stress serve other than a counterproductive one? There is no positive purpose. The first step is to embrace the fact that to a very large extent (except through the uses of the techniques you learn in this book), you cannot ultimately control or change the outcome. You can only do the best you can and then effectively deal with the consequences.

Looking at it another way, if you are ultimately going to pass the test, then it makes no sense to worry about it. If you are not going to pass the test, for slightly different reasons, it also makes no sense to worry about it. So don't!

E. Developing Discipline and Decisiveness.

A substantial requirement for developing confidence and eliminating fear is becoming disciplined and decisive. As stated previously, these are learned, or acquired, traits and not genetic, or inbred. It is also important to understand that discipline and decisiveness are very much related.

While there are three subcategories of discipline (in the context of test preparation) discussed in this chapter, the first is closely tied to decisiveness. This first category of discipline is the discipline to be decisive—that is, the discipline and decisiveness, when confronted with an option, to consistently select the best option without hesitation or distraction. The second subcategory of discipline is time management discipline—that is, the ability to dedicate the time and effort required to accomplish the mission without procrastination or distraction. The third subcategory of discipline is perseverance discipline—that is, the ability to gain and maintain the never quit mentality.

What this book will teach you is the ability to be disciplined and decisive in answering multiples choice examination questions. Through the discipline to be decisive, time management discipline, and perseverance discipline, you will possess all the traits necessary to conquer the multiple-choice exam. You will consistently, and without hesitation, apply systems and principles I have developed to find and mark the best answer every time, even when the best answer is not otherwise jumping out at you. So, for purposes of this chapter, what you need to learn, adopt, and embrace are the basic concepts of decisiveness and the three subcategories of discipline as they apply to preparing for the test.

The Marine Corps teaches a very basic concept on decision making. The concept allows the decision maker to select the single *best* option each and every time by simply applying one qualifier. That qualifier, which clearly identifies the best option, is to select the option that leaves you the most options.

So, for example, if you had a choice of taking one of the three paths, which path would you take? Your choices are as follows: Path A, which leads to Destination A (a beautiful vacation spot); Path B, which leads to Destination B (a great job opportunity); Path C, which leads to Destination C (a place where you will be handed a million dollars); or Path D, which leads to Destination D (a kick in the pants *and* the ability to choose Paths A, B, C, and D at any point in time).

While most people would select A, B, or C (not wanting a kick in the pants), the fact remains that D is clearly the best choice, because it allows you to select any of the other options later, including D (on the off chance you could later use a good kick in the pants).

However, the point here is that you must train yourself to have the discipline and decisiveness to select the best answer, even when it goes against your emotional best choice. Even if you can see the advantage of the additional choices, most people will lack the discipline and go with the emotional response. In this case, vacation looks good, I need the work, or I could use the money. Technically, those are the *wrong* answers. With discipline and the systems set forth in this book, you will select the correct answer and conquer the exam.

On well-crafted multiple-choice examinations, many answer choices are designed to lure you into selecting them. They are designed to create confusion and indecisiveness. In order to stay focused, avoided fear and stress, and to stay on task, you must be decisive and select the best intellectual choice and *not* the best emotional choice. In later chapters, I will show you how exactly to do that. But for purposes of this chapter, understand that becoming decisive and disciplined prior to taking the exam and remaining disciplined and decisive throughout the preparation for and taking of the exam will help you master and pass the exam.

As previously stated, discipline is a concept and topic very much related to decisiveness. However, in addition to having discipline in the way you approach responding to choices and selecting the correct answer on a multiple-choice test (which is the discipline to be decisive), you must also have discipline in the way in which you prepare for taking a multiple-choice exam. This is what I referred to previously as time management discipline. The preparation methods that are described later are not only critical to properly and thoroughly intellectually preparing for the exam, but they are also critical in developing and maintaining the confidence necessary to eliminate fear and all of the by-products of fear.

The third aspect of discipline is the never quit attitude, which is inherent in all successful people. My middle son, Joey Thompson, is likely the best example of this concept. Very much like me, Joey is an intelligent individual with certain learning disabilities. He is easily distracted and has significant difficulties focusing when taking a multiple-choice test in a classroom or other structured environment. If you verbally ask him a difficult question concerning a complex topic that he has studied, he can typically give you a very thorough and correct answer. However, if you put the same question in a formal written test with three other choices, he will not do nearly as well.

While Joey may not pass a test the first time, he will eventually pass it. That is because Joe is mentally tough. He is not one to cry over failure or wince at pain. If he fails, he simply puts his head down and goes at it again. That character trait of perseverance discipline is critical in mentally and emotionally preparing for a multiple-choice exam.

So the point here is that you must acquire and maintain perseverance discipline and the never quit attitude. Once you truly come to grips with the idea that even if you fail, you can try again (which, as previously stated, is the case with the vast majority of standardized multiple-choice tests relating to academic admissions and professional licensure and certification), you will have the confidence necessary to master and ultimately pass the exam. Additionally, in the unlikely event you do fail the exam on your first attempt, the stress and disappointment of that event is significantly diminished, and your likelihood of success on the next try is going to be substantially increased.

Chapter 3

Intellectually Preparing to Attack and Beat the Exam

Step One: Using the Right Exam Preparation Courses

A. Using Focused Memorization.

The first step in good test preparation is to recognize the two resources that you need the most and frequently have the least. Those resources are time and memory space. Unfortunately, most individuals fail to effectively use these resources by either cramming or power reading. Both methods typically fail to yield good results, especially when studying for a comprehensive multiple-choice exam.

Cramming, or the attempt to prepare for a test through rote memorization of limited testable materials over a short period of time immediately preceding the test itself, is rarely effective. In fact, for most people, cramming is a study methodology that is a formula for disaster, especially if the multiple-choice test is a comprehensive exam covering volumes of material. Likewise, power reading, or the reading of the sum total of all information that may be on the test over time and without focus in the hope of ultimately absorbing everything that might be covered, is equally ill advised.

In fact, the single best method of preparing and studying for a multiple-choice exam is what I call focused memorization. This is the method of: (1) identifying what information is going to be tested, (2) determining from the experts on that particular exam the best study method and time line, and (3) following that method and time line using the additional techniques you will learn in this book.

B. Selecting the Right Prep Course.

It is a good idea to complete some type of formal examination preparation course prior to taking a standardized multiple-choice exam. No single bit of advice could be more critical than that. For nearly every standardized multiple-choice examination, there are dozens of these types of courses; they can be classroom-based, web-based, or self-study.

While a formal classroom course of study is typically best, other methods are appropriate either as a good alternative or as a complementary resource to a formal course. The first step is obviously to determine the best preparation course to take. If the multiple-choice examination is an academic aptitude test, such as the ACT, SAT, GRE, GMAT, or LSAT, you should seek the advice and opinions of your school counselors. If the multiple-choice examination is a professional licensing or certification exam, you should seek the advice and opinions of individuals you know who have recently taken and successfully passed that particular examination. If the examination is a licensing examination that is typically taken after completion of a comprehensive course of study (such as the bar examination or the National Registry Paramedic Examination), you should seek the advice and opinion of instructors and administrators of that school.

You should also take advantage of the Internet and review the course, its track record, statistical success rate, and other relevant factors. Another good method of indentifying the best formal exam preparation course is to determine how long it has been offered and how frequently it is offered. While not always foolproof, it is usually safe to assume that if a course has been around for years and is offered several times throughout the year, it is probably a very good course. Not only because the laws of supply and demand would suggest that if it were not a good course, the company offering it would be out of business, but also because most bigger, more successful preparation courses have better intelligence gathering and research capabilities. This means that these companies are typically better able to provide you with a more specific focus on precisely what topics and information is likely to be on the test.

C. Maximizing the Value of the Prep Course.

Once you have selected a test preparation course, you should contact the organization offering that course and find out four important things. First, what do they recommend on the issue of timing between completing their course and taking the exam. While some courses recommend that you take the exam immediately following completion of their course, or as soon thereafter as possible, others may recommend some period of time between their course and taking the test, often to allow for the completion of some post-course exercises or assignments. This information is critical in determining when to schedule both the course and the test.

The second item of information you should obtain is what, if any, course study they recommend or require to be completed in addition to their formal classroom study. For example, many test preparation courses have a prestudy book and/or preexams. It is important to understand this information so that you can properly schedule the course around any prestudy time requirements.

The third item of information you should obtain is whether the course has any afterhours study requirements or homework. This is important to know when scheduling the course to ensure you have adequate time available to complete both in-class and after-class work.

The fourth item of information is whether they recommend the use of any additional study programs. While some formal courses encourage the completion of self-study books or Internet-based courses and/or practice exams in addition to completing their courses, others strongly discourage it. These companies are in the business of helping students successfully pass exams and are usually pretty adept at it, so I would strongly encourage you to follow their advice on these issues.

D. Taking Practice or Sample Tests.

Typically, any formal prep course will come with one or more practice or sample test. I would strongly encourage you to take maximum advantage of this great opportunity and preparation method. As discussed later in this chapter, identifying what is likely to be on the test and what the testing authority is actually looking for is key. Good sample or practice exams will do a great job of teaching you precisely that. Taking several sample or practice exams will also help increase your comfort with the test-taking process and reduce your pretest anxiety. Finally, sample or practice tests will teach you time management, which is also key.

Prior to taking your first practice test, you should determine how many questions will be on the actual test (the real test, not the practice one you will be taking here) and how much time you will have to complete the test. From there, you should be able to calculate how much time you will have on average to complete each question. While taking the practice or sample tests, you should closely monitor your time and make sure that each question is not taking more than the allotted *per question* time limit to answer. If you find yourself taking too much time, move on to the next question.

You should also apply the principles you will learn later in this book on attacking and answering questions when taking practice exams. I recommend you take practice exams from multiple sources. For example, if your preparation course offers several practice exams, you should complete those, as well as others on Internet sites and/or from test preparation books.

E. Using Flash Cards.

Using flash cards can be an invaluable multiple-choice preparation tool, especially if your examination has a vast volume of fairly short and simple concepts that can be easily memorized through continuous exposure to the material. Flash cards are especially useful if you have a study partner or friend, even if he or she is not taking the test but is willing to assist you in your study program.

However, just like with the line out system of study, which we will discuss later in Chapter 5, it is important to reduce the number of flash cards you are studying with over time. This is done by simply removing the cards that contain knowledge you understand and have effectively committed to memory from the study deck. For example, if you begin with three hundred flash cards and, after the first run-through, you determine you understand and have committed to memory the information contained on sixty-six of the cards, remove those sixty-six cards from the deck and continue studying from the remaining 234. If you have eight-four memorized thereafter, remove those eighty-four and continue studying from the remaining 150, and so on until you are out of cards.

F. Using Study Aid Books.

Most standardized multiple-choice tests have one or more published study aid books written on the topic of how to study for and pass that particular exam. These books are typically available online or in book stores. It has been my consistent experience that while these books can occasionally be somewhat effective and helpful, they are more often ineffective and harmful. The information contained in these books is usually dated by at least a year or two, depending on the date of publication. Since standardized tests are typically modified regularly, even good information contained in these books becomes old and, therefore, outdated. That is why I strongly recommend the use of formal preparation courses in lieu of these books, as these courses, like the exams they are preparing students for, are updated regularly and deal in real time.

In summary, while some of these books may ultimately complement other effective study systems, many will overload you with nontestable information or even misguide and confuse you. Accordingly, I do not recommend their use unless a formal exam preparation course for the particular test is unavailable. If you are contemplating purchasing and using one of these books anyway, then you should make sure to read them *before* you take the professional study course and *not* during or after the course.

Chapter 4

Preparing Intellectually to Attack and Beat the Exam

Step Two: Establishing an Effective Study Method and Schedule.

A. Establishing a Good Study Schedule Around the Prep Course.

Now that you have selected a good formal test preparation course, begin working around their recommended time line. For example, if they recommend that you complete a precourse study book and a pretest prior to commencing the formal classroom study, get the materials early and make sure you spend the time and effort necessary in advance of the course to get it completed. If the course requires after-hours study or homework, make sure you schedule time to do it and then actually complete the work.

Whenever possible, schedule the prep course at a time when you will be both well rested and relaxed. Even more important than effective use of time is the use of an effective study method. Most good test preparation courses not only provide you with the information you should expect on the exam but also helpful tips on how to prepare for and take the exam. You should follow this expert advice without exception. For example, if the exam prep instructor tells you to take a week between the course and the test, and during that week, you should review Chapters 1 and 2 of the study materials on Monday, study Chapter 4 on

Tuesday, take Wednesday off, and then study Chapters 3 and 5 on Thursday, make sure you do *precisely* that.

B. Setting Up a Study Schedule in the Absence of a Prep Course.

If you are taking a preparatory course, set your study schedule around the course as previously discussed. In the event that a preparatory course is not available for your examination, then make sure you give yourself enough time to learn the materials and properly study for the test. Again, there is no better resource for obtaining information on a test that through those who have recently taken and passed that same test. While standardized tests typically contain different questions, the focus of the exam does not typically change. Accordingly, individuals with prior test experience can usually provide you with valuable information about what topics were heavily tested. Do not be afraid to ask these people for assistance, as they are typically sympathetic to your situation, having been in your situation prior to taking the exam. Their advice is typically readily available and can be invaluable.

Once you have identified the sum and substance of what you believe you need to know to pass the test, make sure you set aside sufficient time to properly absorb that information. The first step is to identify the volume of information you need to know. The next step is to determine how much of that information you can absorb on a daily basis. The third step is to then "backward plan" a time line, ensuring that you also contemplate personal emergencies and other distractions, as well as some down time between study days. You should also factor in a few days to complete a general study overview of the materials.

For example, if you have a book with ten chapters and you know you can comfortably study for and absorb one chapter each day, you know that you need a minimum of ten study days to complete your preparation. Contemplating a few days for down time, possible personal emergencies, three days for a general study overview, and a Relax Day (discussed in Chapter 11), you now realize you should plan for and schedule at least seventeen to twenty days prior to the exam date to properly study and prepare for the exam. The next step is to actually calendar those days with specific tasks, counting backward (using the previous example) twenty days.

If the test is on October 21, you would set up the following schedule starting twenty days before the test day as follows:

October 1: study Chapter 1
October 2: study Chapter 2
October 3: downtime or emergency day
October 4: study Chapter 3
October 5: study Chapter 4
October 6: study Chapter 5
October 7: downtime or emergency day
October 8: study Chapter 6
October 9: study Chapter 7
October 10: downtime or emergency day
October 11: study Chapter 8
October 12: study Chapter 9
October 13: study Chapter 10
October 14: downtime or emergency day
October 15: first day of overview: Chapters 1-4
October 16: second day overview: Chapters 5-7
October 17: third day overview: Chapters 8-10
October 18: downtime or emergency day
October 19: final global summary review of all chapters
October 20: relax day and first final review
October 21: second final review and test day

Once you begin the schedule, it is important to revise and update as you go. For example, using the previous study schedule, if on October 3 you are still fresh and do not need a downtime day or emergency day, review Chapter 3 and move all of the remaining days up by one day. The key here is to stay disciplined and focused and remain on schedule. Do not be afraid of getting ahead of schedule. Likewise, using the example schedule, it would be easy to tell yourself on October 5 that you do not really need to review Chapter 4, because you have at least four more downtime days that you may not ever use so you should simply convert that day to an unscheduled downtime day. Making that mistake will likely come back to haunt you if you encounter unexpected emergencies and end up using all of the scheduled downtime days.

The important point here is to stay focused and on task. Resist the urge to procrastinate or lose discipline. It is important that you absolutely stay on schedule. The best example of this concept is my daughter, Katie Thompson. Katie is very good at time management and has the discipline to stay on task. While in college, she was heavily involved in several academic, fraternal, and public service organizations. She also remained employed with multiple jobs throughout the process. However, by establishing time lines and schedules and sticking to them, she still completed a bachelor's degree in four years and a master's degree in two, notwithstanding all the exceptionally challenging and time-consuming distractions.

The point here is to build a realistic study schedule and time line and maintain the focus and discipline to stay both on schedule and on task.

Chapter 5

Preparing Intellectually to Attack and Beat the Exam

Step Three: Focusing on What You Need to Know

A. Recognizing the Difference Between Learning and Proper Test Preparation.

The single biggest mistake made by most people preparing to take a multiple-choice exam is the effort to learn the materials instead of preparing for exam. While some people mistakenly believe this is the same thing, it is often very different. When you are preparing for a multiple-choice test you need to recognize the mission. The mission is NOT to understand and apply the subject matter the real world. The mission is to pass the test, plain and simple.

For example, if you know that a testable topic is simply that the sky is blue, do not bother learning about the various reasons why the sky is blue or all of the occasions when the sky is not blue. Simply memorize the fact the sky is blue and move on to the next testable topic. As stated previously, the two most limited resources available to an individual preparing for an exam are time and memory space, so the rule here is conserve memory space and fill it only with testable items.

B. Focusing on What is Testable and Understanding What the Test is Actually Looking For.

So the first step in studying for the exam is to determine what questions and/or topics are likely to be testable. While you certainly would not want to try to steal a copy of the test and answer sheet, there are legitimate ways of obtaining a more focused understanding of what is likely to be on the test. As stated earlier, the single best way to obtain this type of focus is through a formal test preparation course. Typically, these courses will not only help you study for the exam but will also help you focus on what to study.

If a formal test preparation course is not available, then obtaining that information from prior test takers is your next best option. In seeking out prior test takers, you should look for those individuals who both took the test recently and actually passed the test. When using this method, you should also speak with as many prior test takers as possible so that you have a better consensus on what materials were tested. If one prior test taker tells you that the sky is blue is on the test, then it may very well be. If five prior test takers say so, you can likely count on it. This is especially true considering that many standardized multiple-choice tests use different versions of the test with completely different questions.

The second step is to then focus only on what you need to know to pass the exam. At this step, it is critical to understand what the testing authority is actually looking for. Some testing authorities are looking purely for rote memorization and regurgitation of memorizable facts. Examples of this are most real estate licensing exams and securities registration exams. Others are looking for the ability to demonstrate an understanding and application of the underlying concepts. Examples of this are the attorney bar and paramedic national registry examinations. So if the test falls into the first category (rote memorization of facts), then focus on memorizing the testable facts and do not spend time trying to understand or apply the facts.

Again, the point of the exercise is to pass the test, nothing more. If the test falls into the second category (ability to understand and apply concepts), then do not spend time memorizing facts, but instead focus on understanding and applying the concepts. For example, the focus of the National Registry Board of Examiners for Paramedics is not to simply memorize facts but to obtain and demonstrate an understanding of how the human body works and reacts to disease, trauma, and, ultimately, various medical interventions. So if you were to simply try to memorize every sign and symptom of every disease and type of trauma imaginable, you would likely not pass the exam unless you were a genius with a photographic memory. Instead, to pass the exam, you need to gain an understanding of how the various systems generally react to certain medical conditions. Armed with that information, you can now study and learn what is important and ignore those topics and concepts that have little or no bearing to passing the exam.

C. Limiting the Volume of Knowledge to be Absorbed.

When studying for a multiple-choice exam, the key is to limit the volume of information to be absorbed and then thoroughly absorb that limited information. The single best way to do this is through what I call the highlight and line out system of study. The concept is fairly simple, and it works.

The first step is to go through all of the study outlines you are using and highlight the items of information you need to know for the test. If you do not have outlines, then do this with your study notes. After you have gone through the materials and highlighted everything potentially testable, then go back through the materials a second time, testing yourself on the highlighted areas only. As you go through this exercise, line out the highlighted information you know and understand completely but leave intact the highlighted areas you are not yet fully comfortable with. Then go through the material a third time, reviewing highlighted (and not yet lined out) materials while continuing to line out additional highlighted areas that you feel you have mastered. Continue this exercise until all highlighted areas are lined out.

If the test involves working mathematical formulas, make sure you identify and memorize the formulas you will need to know to pass the exam. If you are allowed to use a calculator, ensure that you know exactly how to calculate the formulas on the calculator you will be using for the exam. Since many calculators have different functions and methods for inputting data and calculating solutions based on formulas, make sure you are well practiced and know the formulas and your calculator cold. Trying to learn your calculator or how to calculate formulas during the exam is a formula for disaster.

When studying for a multiple-choice exam, it is also important to understand the intrinsic values of certain types of questions and focus on those that bring the most value. For example, certain types of test questions may have a higher point value. In that case, you should focus on and truly master the information likely to be contained in those higher-point questions.

Likewise, certain questions may come with a time commitment that makes them not worth answering. A good example of this is the mathematical calculation of bond duration in the CFP exam. The instructor in the preparatory course I took for that exam noted that the calculation of bond duration takes, on average, approximately nine minutes to complete. The average time allotment you have for each question on that exam is approximately two minutes. So, in sum, spending time attempting to answer the bond duration question, even if you get it right, will likely cause you to flunk the exam.

There are two learning points here. First, do not spend time attempting to answer questions that, based on point value and the required time to obtain the correct answer, are better simply answered with the default answer (discussed in Chapter 10). Second, do not spend valuable study time and valuable memory space preparing to answer those same questions. Instead, use that time and space to study the information you will need to answer the questions you intend to answer.

Chapter 6

Preparing Intellectually to Attack and Beat the Exam

Step Four: Using Proven Methodsfor Memorizing MaterialsA. Find Easy Ways to Memorize Testable Items.

To the extent you must commit certain information to rote memory in order to pass the exam, it is very important to find and use memory hooks relating to that information. That will much better facilitate the ability of your brain to retrieve and recall data. The three best methods to do this are through the development and use of acronyms, the development and use of other memory aids, and the recognition of similarities or consistencies.

Acronyms are simply words that are made up of initials that each stand for something. An example of a common acronym is the word *radar*, which stands for Radio Detection And Ranging. Acronyms are best utilized when attempting to memorize a number of terms or concepts that are tied to a common concept or theme. You would simply take the first letter of each of the multiple terms or concepts and then create a word or phrase with those letters. So, as a simple example, if you needed to memorize that the colors of the rainbow are red, orange, yellow, green, blue, indigo, and violet, you would need to find a word (real or made up) or phrase that contains the letters R, O, Y, G, B, I, and V. One example would be to remember when it comes to testing on the colors of rainbows, GIVe ROY a B. The additional advantage of this memory aid is that in attempting to come up with acronyms, you typically begin to automatically memorize the underlying concepts.

Other memory aids would include finding ways to relate a concept or rule to something you can relate to personally. For example, if you needed to remember that a checkerboard has sixty-four squares, you would want to think about something personal to you that relates to the number sixty-four. For example, if your mother is sixty-four years old, then remember "old Mom likes to play checkers." When you see the question, you would remember her age and know it is sixty-four. A real-world example would be attempting to memorize the six ADLs (activities of daily living), which is a medical insurance concept. Most individuals studying for the state health insurance exam will simply spend time memorizing that actual six ADLs, which are: transferring (getting out of bed), toileting, bathing, dressing, eating, and maintaining continence. Instead, it becomes a great deal simpler to simply think about the first six things you do when you wake up in the morning, which are get out of bed, use the toilet, take a shower, get dressed, eat breakfast, and use the bathroom again before you leave the house.

A third memory aid is to recognize similarities or consistencies and use those to memorize multiple concepts. For example, on the paramedic exam, you are heavily tested in the area of human anatomy. One concept you need to know is which sides of the heart the tricuspid (three) valve and bicuspid (two) valve are located. You would also need to know how many lobes are contained in the left and right sides of the lungs. So if you think of "left two" and "right three," you would then easily remember that the tricuspid value is on the right side of the heart, and the right lung has three lobes, while the bicuspid valve is on the left side of the heart, and the left lung has two lobes. Not only does this concept save time and memory space, but also better commits that information from the short-term to the long-term memory.

Once you have developed all of your memory hooks, you need to develop a cheat sheet. A cheat sheet is one or two pages that include all of your memory hooks, any formulas you need to know for the exam, and any items that remain highlighted from the highlight and line out system previously discussed (those items that you are having difficulty committing to memory). This will be used for your final review.

Unfortunately, however, there is only one way to study and memorize math formulas, and that is to practice, practice, practice until doing the formula is second nature. Because some math problems can be calculated in different ways, find the method that works best for you. If you have a system that works, even if it is nonstandard and unorthodox, use *your* system.

Chapter 7

Attacking the Test: Disecting the Question

A. Givens, Maybes, and Defaults.

Going back to basic Marine Corps concepts, you have to focus on one thing and one thing only, and that is accomplishing the mission. What is the mission here? In the simplest of terms, the mission is to past the test. The mission is *not* to demonstrate your mastery of the topics, and it isn't to show the world you understand the materials. It is merely to systematically answer as many questions correctly as you can in the time allotted.

So with that, let's begin by noting that there are only three types of questions you can encounter—those you know the correct answer to (givens), those you are fairly certain you know the answer to (maybes), and those you do not know the answer to (defaults). If you follow my systems set forth in the following chapters, you will be assured of getting 100 percent of the givens, greater than 50 percent of the maybes, and about 30 percent of the defaults. That math should allow you to successfully pass the exam!

The problem with givens is that many test takers assume they will get 100 percent of the givens right, but in fact, they rarely, if ever, do. This is because many test takers make two fatal mistakes. They either fail to properly manage time and therefore never get to read and correctly answer several of the givens, or they fail to carefully read the question and respond incorrectly as a result. It is this issue that will be addressed in this chapter.

The problem with maybes, like givens, is that many maybes are lost in the same time management or failure to read the question problem encountered with givens. Finally, while credit for defaults can also be lost through these problems, credit for defaults are far more frequently lost in the process of selecting answers, which will be addressed in a later chapter.

B. Properly Reading and Classifying the Question.

There are three steps to properly reading and classifying, and thereby being able to correctly answer, a test question. The first step is to obtain a very general understanding the question. The second step is to understand the extent or limitations of the question. Extent and limitations of a question are the use of words such as always, never, usually, sometimes, may, shall, only, not, first, last, or any other word that qualifies, limits, or focuses the object of the question. Identifying and understanding the extent and limitation words in a question is important, as they can completely change the meaning of a question. The third step is to classify the question, once understood, as a given, maybe, or default.

So the first step is to quickly read through the question to understand what the question generally appears be asking. The second step is to then reread the question and highlight each important word and each word of extent or limitation.

Consider the following question:

Trevor and Katie lived in North Carolina. Trevor picked ten apples and five oranges. Trevor decided to give Katie all of the fruit, not including the oranges. How many pieces of fruit did Trevor give Katie?

After initially reading the question, you realize this is simply about the math and fruit and has nothing to do with North Carolina. You also realize there are words of extent and limitation that affect this question. So you reread the question and highlight as follows:

Trevor and Katie lived in North Carolina. Trevor picked <u>ten</u> <u>apples</u> and <u>five oranges</u>. Trevor decided to give Katie <u>all</u> of the <u>fruit</u> <u>not</u> including the <u>oranges</u>. <u>How many pieces of fruit did</u> <u>Trevor give Katie?</u>

In the previous example, a simple given question could be answered incorrectly if not read carefully and the words *all* or *not* were missed. In addition, by highlighting the important information in the question, it will save you valuable time if you mark the question for review and return to review the question later.

C. Classifying the Question as a Given, Maybe, or Default and Responding Accordingly.

The next step is to categorize the question. Once you have completed step one and have reviewed and highlighted the question, and *before* you look at the possible answers, determine whether you believe you know the answer. *Then* review the optional answers. At this point, you can easily categorize the question into one of the following three categories:

The following questions are givens:

1. The answer you thought was correct before reviewing the possible answers does appear as one of those answers.
2. The answer you thought was correct before reviewing the possible answers does *not* appear as one of those answers, but after reviewing the possible answers, you are confident one of those is in fact the correct answer.
3. You did not know the answer prior to reviewing the possible answers, but after reviewing the answers, you are confident one of those is in fact the correct answer.

The following questions are maybes:

1. After reviewing the answers, you are somewhat confident but are not completely confident that one of those is, in fact, the correct answer.
2. After reviewing the answers, you can confidently eliminate all but two of the answers.

The following questions are defaults:

1. Any question that you have not categorized as either a given or a maybe.

Once you have categorized a question as a given, maybe, or default, you can then answer the question based on the procedures set forth in Chapters 8 and 9.

D. Managing your Time.

As stated previously, managing your time during the test is critical to passing the test. If you know how many questions will be on the test and how much time you have to complete the test before you arrive at the test site, then you should have already calculated how much time you have to spend on each question. Accordingly, you should be monitoring your time to ensure you stay on pace.

If you do not have the necessary information prior to arriving, take a minute to calculate the time you have per question after arrival and, if necessary, even after the test begins. Since valuable time can be used up simply checking the clock, I recommend that you calculate how many questions you should be answering in ten minutes and then check the clock as soon as you have completed that number of questions. For example, if you determine that you need to complete each question in two minutes or less, check the clock after five questions (two minutes for each of five questions is ten minutes) and see if you are on time. If you are lagging behind, you will need to speed up the process.

Also, if your test has certain questions that are worth more points than others, make sure you focus on those questions and, if possible, begin with those questions. However, common sense must also be applied to this rule in recognizing an exception. If the higher value questions are far more difficult or time-consuming, do not sacrifice points here. For example, if you have forty-four questions worth two points and four questions worth three points, and the four-point questions are twice as difficult and take more than twice the time to answer, then you should focus on the forty-four two-point questions and *not* the four three pointers.

Finally, make sure you do not run out of time before *all* questions are answered. Once you are at a point in which the remaining time is just enough to allow you to go back and mark *all* remaining unanswered questions with your default answer, stop answering questions and complete all unanswered questions by marking your default answer so that no question is left blank.

Chapter 8

Attacking the Test: Responding With an Answer

A. Marking Questions for Review.

In this chapter you will learn, among other things, how to effectively use the mark for review concept to help master the exam. The inherent advantage of taking a paper test (as opposed to a computer-based test) is that you have the ability to leave certain questions unanswered and then go back to those questions later once you have otherwise completed the exam. It is also easy on a paper test to "mark for review" certain questions that you are uncertain of but have answered anyway. That way, you can easily identify those questions later when you go back to revisit and reconsider the answers you were previously uncertain of.

Likewise, the problem with many computer-based tests is that they do not allow for questions to be left unanswered or for the test taker to go back and revisit previous answers. However, the computer tests that do allow you to leave questions unanswered or to reconsider questions previously answered typically have a "mark for review" function. In other words, you can electronically identify these questions up front and then go back later, via the computer program, directly to the questions you've marked.

If the computer test you are taking allows for you to go back and revisit previously answered questions but does not have a mark for review function, you should create your own mark for review program by simply keeping track of those questions on a piece of scratch paper. It is important to note that if the computer-based test you are taking does not allow you to revisit previously answered questions, then there is no point in leaving any question unanswered or marking questions for review.

B. Responding to Givens and Defaults.

If you have categorized a question as a given, then mark the answer and go to the next question. If you have categorized a question as a default, select your default answer (discussed in Chapter 9), mark the question for review by placing a mark next to the question either with your pencil (if you have a paper test) or electronically (if you are taking a computer test), and then go to the next question. If the question is a default in which the default answer is an answer you are *certain* is incorrect, then and only then should you leave the default question unanswered, mark for review, and go to the next question. Of course, if you are taking a computer test that does not allow you to go back to prior questions, you would not leave any questions unanswered. In that circumstance, you would answer these questions using the logical guessing techniques you will learn in Chapter 10.

C. Responding to a Maybe.

If you have categorized a question as a maybe, then you will either answer the question or skip the question depending on which subcategory of *maybe* the question falls under. If the question is a maybe because you are somewhat confident, but not completely confident, about one of the answers (Type I maybe), then select that answer you believe to be correct, do *not* mark the question for review, and go to the next question.

Alternatively, if the question is a maybe because you have confidently eliminated all but two of the answers (Type II maybe), then there is a three-step process to be followed. The first step in determining which of the two possible answers to select is based upon what the testing authority is looking for. Consider the goals and preferences of the testing authority and then apply those principles to the two answer options to determine which one is the better answer. Some real-world examples of the previous principle are as follows.

The Certified Financial Planner Board is well known to be very conservative regarding recommending investments to clients. So if the two possible answers on the CFP exam were: "A. Recommend a high-yield, high-risk portfolio" or "B. Recommend a moderate-yield, moderate-risk portfolio," the answer would be B. Because that answer is more conservative, it is more consistent with the testing authority's preferences.

Likewise, it is well known that the National Registry of Paramedics stresses the application of basic medical interventions before more advanced medical interventions. So if the two possible answers on the paramedic exam were: "A. Clear the airway and check breathing and circulation" or "B. Intubate and administer drugs," the answer would be A. The first option involves a more basic set of interventions and is more consistent with the testing authority's preferences.

If you can select the best answer from two possible answers based on the testing authority's preferences, then select that answer, do *not* mark the question for review, and go to the next question.

If the first step does not lead you to the correct answer, then the second step is to apply the "intelligent guessing" concepts you will learn in Chapter 10. If you have still failed to identify the correct answer after completing these two steps, the third step is to determine whether or not one of the two possible answers is your default answer. If it is, then select the default answer, mark the question for review, and go to the next question. If neither of the two possible answers is your default answer, then leave the question unanswered, mark the question for review, and then go to the next question.

D. Reviewing Questions.

After you have answered all of the exam questions pursuant to the previously described guidelines, unless every question was a given, you will now have both unanswered and answered questions marked for review. The next step is to begin with the unanswered questions.

By definition, there are only two types of questions that should be initially left unanswered. The first are maybes in which you were able to eliminate all but two of the answers but could not decide based on testing authority preference or intelligent guessing, and neither of the options was your default answer. The second are defaults in which you are certain the default answer is not correct but are unsure of the other three answers. In the case of these questions, simply reread each question as highlighted. If the question becomes a given, mark that answer and go to the next unanswered question. If you remain unsure, then review your prior two choices (or three in the case of an unanswered default), simply select your best guess (avoiding answer A for the statistical reasons you will learn about in Chapter 9), and go to the next unanswered question.

Once you have answered all of the previously unanswered questions, begin reviewing the maybes and defaults you answered but marked for review. Let me begin here by stating that I do not challenge the long-standing rule that you should never change a test answer once you have answered it. In fact, in my personal experience taking well over a thousand multiple-choice exams, I cannot recall a single time I changed an answer from one guess to another guess that did not turn out to be a mistake. However, I do believe there is one exception, and that is when you subsequently conclude, to an absolute certainty and by virtue of some new information obtained from another question, that a previous answer is incorrect and the new selection is correct.

So with respect to the answered questions marked for review, simply reread the question and your answer, and unless you are absolutely certain, based on information obtained from another question, that another answer is in fact correct, leave the answer unchanged. If you are certain about the merits of the change, then, and only then, should you consider changing your answer.

An example of a changeable answer would be as follows. In response to the question "Which of the following colors is not a color of the rainbow? A. Red, B. Green, C. Purple, D. Indigo," you mark Indigo, because you know for certain that red and green are rainbow colors. But then a subsequent question states "Which colors of the rainbow fall between red and indigo?" which establishes the fact that indigo is, like red and green, a wrong answer and confirms that purple is the correct answer. Absent something this clear, *do not change answers.*

Finally, if you begin to run out of time before you have answered all questions and you must simply guess all remaining answers, simply mark all unanswered questions with the default answer.

E. Dealing with Multiple-Option Questions.

Many standardized multiple-choice tests now use multiple-option questions. Those are questions that include several statements of fact along with answers that suggest groups of those statements are correct or incorrect. The following is an example of a multiple-option question:

Susie has 12 apples, 8 oranges, and 4 pears. Susie gives half the apples to Ronnie and the remainder of her fruit to Joey. Based on the foregoing, which of the following statements is correct:

1. Susie has 6 apples
2. Ronnie has 12 pears
3. Joey has no pears
4. Susie has no oranges

A. 1 and 3 are correct
B. 2 and 4 are correct
C. 1, 2, and 3 are correct
D. 1 and 4 are correct

Many test takers dislike this form of question, because they believe that the complexity of this form makes it more difficult to answer correctly and takes more time to work through, hence wasting valuable test time. However, they can, in fact, be simpler if you approach them correctly.

Let's begin by looking at how *not* to attack this form of question. The typical test taker would look at the previous sample question and approach it as follows:

Step one: Read the question and statements 1-4.

Step two: Read optional answer A.

Step three: Go back and review statements 1 and 3.

Step four: Compare statement 1 to the question and determine whether it is true or false.

Step five: Realizing that statement 1 is true (so answer A may still be the correct answer), then compare statement 3 to the question and determine whether it is true or false.

Step six: Realizing that statement 3 is incorrect (so answer A is incorrect), read optional answer B.

Step seven: Go back and review statements 2 and 4.

Step eight: Compare statement 2 to the question and determine whether it is true or false.

Step nine: Realizing that statement 2 is incorrect (so B is incorrect), read optional answer C

Step ten: Go back and review statements 1, 2, and 3.

Step eleven: Compare statement 1 to the question and determine whether it is true or false.

Step twelve: Realizing that statement 1 is true (so answer C may still be the correct answer), then compare statement 2 to the question and determine whether it is true or false.

Step thirteen: Realizing that statement 2 is incorrect (so C is incorrect), read optional answer D.

Step fourteen: Go back and review statements 1 and 4.

Step fifteen: Compare statement 1 to the question and determine whether it is true or false.

Step sixteen: Realizing that statement 1 is true (so answer D may still be the correct answer), then compare statement 4 to the question and determine whether it is true or false.

Step seventeen: Realizing that statement 4 is also correct (so answer D is the correct answer), select answer D.

There are several real problems with the foregoing process. First, we have just taken a very simple question that should take no more than thirty seconds to answer correctly and turned it into a complex, two-minute evolution. Second, we have spent valuable time and mental energy we could have been using to correctly answer the next question. Third, by creating twelve additional and unnecessary steps in the process (three times more steps), you have significantly increased your likelihood of making a mistake and turning a given into a wrong answer.

Here is the correct method to approach that same multiple option question:

Step one: Read the question.

Step two: Read statement 1 and compare it to the question. If it is incorrect, line it out and then also line out every answer that indicates statement 1 is correct. (In the example, nothing is lined out yet.)

Step three: Read statement 2 and compare it to the question. If it is incorrect, line it out and then also line out every answer that indicates statement 2 is correct. (In the example, statement 2 and answers B and C are lined out.)

Step four: Read statement 3 and compare it to the question. If it is incorrect, line it out and then also line out every answer that indicates statement 3 is correct. (In the example, statement 3 and answers A is lined out.)

Step five: Select Answer D as the only remaining possible answer and go to the next question.

We have just eliminated twelve unnecessary and time-consuming steps and made a complex two-minute process a simple thirty-second process, while also decreasing the likelihood of a costly mistake being made in the process.

E. Summarizing the System.

So now that you have learned the system for responding to givens, maybes, and defaults, let's summarize the system.

1. Givens (you know the answer):

    A. Mark that answer;
    B. Do *not* mark for review;
    C. Go to the next question.

2. Type I Maybe (you are somewhat confident about one of the answers but it is *not* a given):

    A. Mark that answer;

    B. Do *not* mark for review;

    C. Go to the next question.

3. Type II Maybe (you have confidently eliminated all but two of the answers):

    A. Mark the answer most consistent with testing authority preference;

    B. Mark the best answer based on intelligent guessing (if testing authority preference did not give you the answer)"

    C. Do *not* mark for review;

    D. Go to the next question.

4. Type II Maybe (when you cannot select an option based upon testing authority preference or intelligent guessing, and one of the two possible answers is your default answer):

    A. Mark your default answer;

    B. Mark for review;

    C. Go to the next question;

    D. Return to the question after exam completion;

    E. Change the answer only if a different answer is now a given;

    F. Go to the next review question.

5. Type II Maybe (when you cannot select an option based upon testing authority preference or intelligent guessing, and neither of the two possible answers is your default answer):

    A. Leave the question unanswered;

    B. Mark the question for review;

    C. Go to the next question;

    D. Return to the question after exam completion;

    E. If the question is now a given, mark that answer;

    F. If not a given, select your best guess; G. Go to the next review question.

6. Default (question is neither a given nor a maybe):

    A. Unless you are absolutely sure the default answer is incorrect, mark your default answer;
    B. Mark the question for review;
    C. Return to the question after exam completion; D. Change the answer only if a different answer is now a given;
    D. Go to the next review question.

7. Default (when you are absolutely sure the default answer is incorrect):

    A. Leave the question unanswered;
    B. Mark the question for review;
    C. Go to the next question;
    D. Return to the question after exam completion;
    E. If the question is now a given, mark that answer;
    F. If not a given, select your best guess;
    G. Go to the next review question.

8. Finally, let's summarize the overall procedure:

    A. Answer all questions that can be answered the first time through;
    B. Return to the *unanswered* questions marked for review and answer those next;
    C. Return to the *answered* questions marked for review and change them *only* if they have become a givens.

Chapter 9

Playing the Odds: Using Statistics and Chance to Your Advantage

As stated previously, you have to focus on one thing and one thing only, and that is accomplishing the mission. Once again, the mission here is to systematically answer as many questions correctly as you can in the time allotted. If you follow the systems discussed so far, you will be assured of getting 100 percent of the givens. So now let's focus on obtaining greater than 50 percent of the maybes and about 30 percent of the defaults.

A. Understanding the Rules of the Game.

The word *game* is defined as "competitive activity involving skill, chance, or endurance on the part of two or more persons who play according to a set of rules, usually for their own amusement or for that of spectators." While many may debate with the author whether and to what extent multiple-choice exams are prepared by testing authorities to some extent for their own amusement, there is no question that it is a competitive activity involving skill and chance on the part of two or more persons who play according to a set of rules.

Accordingly, since we have now established that multiple-choice testing is nothing more than a game of chance and skill, it is important to understand the rules of the game. Unfortunately, in the game of multiple-choice exams, your opponent (the testing authority) gets to set all the rules and change them at will. Consequently, we, as disadvantaged opponents, must use proven systems, based on math and statistics, to gain the advantage and win the game.

When answering a multiple-choice question in which you are uncertain of the answer, the game becomes a game of chance. Consequently, not unlike playing blackjack in a casino, you must play according to proven systems that rely on math and statistics in order to increase your odds. More importantly, you have to stay disciplined and consistently answer questions according to those systems even when all of your instincts and even common sense tell you not to. Especially when, in the case of multiple-choice exams *and* blackjack, you do not have to win every time, you just have to win most of the time.

My youngest son, Trevor Stewart, is an exceptionally disciplined individual. A three-time high school state champion wrestler and nationally ranked Division I college wrestler, he can always maintain the discipline required to accomplish the task or goal he sets his sights on. I watched him train like a Navy Seal while going days without food or water to make weight for an upcoming match. In sum, temptation was always trumped by the rules he set for himself. He is also a very proficient blackjack player for the exact same reasons. When confronted with a difficult decision in which his instincts and common sense tell him to take another card, he resists the urge to "go with his gut" and instead plays by the established rules and proven systems. While, based purely on chance, he may not win every blackjack hand he plays, he will, based on the applicable laws of math and statistics, win more frequently by having the discipline to follow the rules.

In taking and passing multiple-choice exams, just like with blackjack, if you have the discipline to follow the systems every time, you will win most of the time.

❧

49

B. Following the Rules and Winning the Game.

In Chapters 2 and 4 we spent a great deal of time discussing the values of discipline and decisiveness. Discipline and decisiveness allow you to fully and properly prepare for the exam—physically, mentally, and emotionally. Discipline and decisiveness also allow you to develop a study schedule and stick to it. However, at the end of the day, discipline and decisiveness are most critical here, in having the discipline and decisiveness to follow the systems contained in this book when actually taking the test and selecting an answer.

Let's beginning by discussing why most multiple-choice test takers tend to be their own worst enemies. Most people have a natural tendency to doubt themselves and to second-guess their decisions, no matter how certain they were when they made the initial decision. Regardless of the level of knowledge you have on the materials and how confident you are going into the test, you will have some level of doubt on almost every answer you select. This is partly due to human nature and in even larger part due to the fact that almost every testing authority sets out to trick you in the testing.

Whether the reason for this is to ensure that those who ultimately pass the applicable test have clear mastery and understanding of the subject matter (which is the position taken by most testing authorities) or because they want to make sure those following in their footsteps are forced to face a much more difficult challenge then they had to face to achieve the same results (which is the position of many test takers and this author), the fact remains that most standardized multiple-choice tests are built to confuse and trick the test taker. Their game is to get you to doubt yourself and thereby get you to break the established rules. Resist the urge to play their game. Instead, win the game by playing by your rules, not theirs. ●

C. Understanding and Applying the Concept of the Default Answer.

In order to embrace and apply the concept of the default answer, you must understand the concept. Studies on multiple-choice exams have consistently proven two concepts. The first concept is that if you randomly select or guess the answer to a specified number of questions, you will generally get less than 25 percent of the answers correct. Alternatively, if you consistently select the *same* letter answer on each random selection, then assuming that each letter answer (A, B, C, or D) is used throughout the test in an equal fashion, you will, by definition, obtain a 25 percent success rate.

The second concept is that in the vast majority of standardized multiple-choice tests involving four possible answers, the letter A is the least utilized answer, being the correct answer far less than 25 percent of the time. In fact, B, C, and D are far more common answers. The logic behind this is because test preparers, as we have already discussed, do not want to make the test easy. They want to make it as difficult and as time-consuming as possible. If the answer is A, the test taker need not read or consider options B, C, or D, and therefore, the question becomes easier, less confusing, less time-consuming, and everything the testing authority does not want it to be.

Now, if you take those two concepts and apply logic and math, it becomes apparent that a test taker is far more likely to increase the number of correctly answered defaults by simply selecting one letter answer as his or her default answer and answering each and every default question with that default answer. The default answer, of course, should be B, C, or D.

Once you pick one of those letters as your default answer, then you must have the discipline to stick with it and answer every default with the default answer. Since B, C, and D are typically used in an exam collectively more than 75 percent of the time and therefore individually more than 25 percent of the time, using this system yields far better results than individual random guessing. Statistically, if your test has twenty-five defaults (questions you cannot narrow to one or two possible answers with some level of certainty), the use of this system will increase your number of correct answers by five or more. That could easily mean the difference between passing and failing.

D. The Concept of Not Changing Answers.

Of course, no book on multiple-choice test taking would be complete without the mention of the rule "do not change answers." Other than the very limited circumstances in which changing an answer makes sense as discussed in Chapter 8, do *not* change answers.

Chapter 10

The Art of Intelligent Guessing: Applying Logicand Common Sense

A. Givens and Defaults, No Time to Guess.

In Chapter 7, we identified the three types of questions on a multiple-choice exam: given, defaults, and maybes. The rules described in that chapter for answering each of these types of questions make clear that the test taker should have very limited opportunities to guess at answers. However, the fact remains that the opportunity to guess, albeit limited, does exist. Accordingly, the purpose of this chapter is to identify systems and methods that maximize your likelihood of success, should you be required to guess.

Briefly reviewing the rules in Chapter 7, there should be no time when you would be required to guess with a given (a question in which you know the answer), a single-answer maybe (a question in which you are fairly certain but not completely certain you know the answer), or a default (a question in which you do not know the answer and cannot confidently narrow the possible correct answers to two). The reason you would not guess with a given is because you know the answer and do need to guess. The reason you would not guess with a single-answer maybe is because your guess would, by definition, be the answer you already believe is correct. The reason you would not guess with a default is because you do not know the answer and will therefore work the odds and answer with your default answer. So, by definition, the only type of question you would guess at is in a multiple-answer maybe—a question that, after reviewing the possible answers, you can confidently eliminate all but two of the answers.

B. The Art of Intelligent Guessing: Same and Different Answers.

If two answers are the same and the question only allows you to select one right answer, then, by definition, both answers must be wrong.

For example, consider the following question:

Katie has a pet named Marley. Marley is a:

A. Cat
B. Lizard
C. Dog
D. Reptile.

Since a lizard is a reptile, answers B and D are the same and therefore cannot be correct. Now to apply the rule to that example. If the above question was a maybe because you knew that Marley was neither a lizard nor a cat and were therefore down to two possible answers (reptile or dog), you could eliminate reptile and correctly guess answer C. Dog.

Likewise, the opposite rule applies for two answers that are opposite. If two answers are opposite, then more than likely, one of them is the correct answer.

Consider the following question:

While Kristy was working at the hospital, she witnessed a patient begin to hemorrhage. The patient is:

A. Choking
B. Bleeding
C. Sweating

D. Not bleeding

Because answers B and D are opposites, by definition, one of them must be correct. Now apply that example to the rule. If that question was a maybe because you knew hemorrhage was either choking or bleeding, you could eliminate choking because you know the answer is likely either B or D. You would therefore correctly choose answer B. Bleeding.

C. The Art of Intelligent Guessing: Very Similar but not the Same Answers.

As stated in the last subsection, if two answers are the same (identical for all intents and purposes) and the question only allows you to select one right answer, then, by definition, both answers must be wrong. However, the opposite is usually true when answers involving a number of facts are very similar. For example, consider the following question:

Ronnie and Katie both like sports. But they disagree about which sports are fun to watch. Which is true about Ronnie and Katie:

A. Ronnie and Katie both love football, wrestling, and golf, but only Ronnie hates tennis.
B. Ronnie and Katie both love football and wrestling, but only Ronnie hates tennis.
C. Ronnie and Katie both love golf and volleyball, but only Katie hates wrestling.
D. Ronnie and Katie both hate football and rugby, but only Katie loves basketball.

When looking at all four answers, it is clear that answers A and B have three out of four identical facts making the answers very similar but not the same (1. Ronnie and Katie love football, 2. Ronnie and Katie love wrestling, and 3. Ronnie hates tennis). Consequently, if you, as the test taker, knew that any one of the three identical facts was incorrect, you could immediately eliminate both answers as possible correct answers. Because test preparers do not want to make answer elimination simple, it is highly unlikely that any of these identical facts are wrong, making one of the very similar answers likely the correct answer. Accordingly, you would eliminate answers C and D.

Next, having narrowed the options to answers A and B, you would look at the one inconsistent fact in those two answers and see if it is stated in one of the previously eliminated answers (thus applying the same logic and finding another similarity). Here, the inconsistent fact is that Ronnie and Katie both love golf, and answer C also notes that Ronnie and Katie both love golf. Because answer A is similar to both B and C, the answer would be A. Conversely, if answer C stated that Ronnie or Katie hated golf, that would make answer B more consistent with C, and thus, answer B would be the likely correct answer.

D. The Art of Intelligent Guessing: Absolutes are Rarely Correct.

Most multiple-choice exams attempt to test your knowledge on real-world facts. Because most facts, even rules, have exceptions, test answers that contain absolutes are typically not correct.

For example, answers with absolute words such as *always* and *never* are typically wrong. On the rare occasion that an always or never concept is applicable, it usually involves a very import concept or rule you would likely remember from your prep course. For that reason, if you see one of these in the context of a question you are not certain of, it is likely not the correct answer.

For example, consider the following question:

Ronnie has a dog named Kodie. The following is true about Ronnie and Kodie:

A. Ronnie paid $100 for Kodie
B. Ronnie always walks Kodie at noon

C. Ronnie bought a dog bed for Kodie
D. Ronnie sold Kodie to his brother Joey

Because answer B contains the absolute word *always*, it is not likely to be the right answer. Now apply the rule to that example. If the question was a maybe because you had eliminated answers A and D, you can also eliminate answer B and correctly guess answer C.

For the same reason that test answers containing absolutes are typically not the correct answer, test answers that contain words of flexibility are usually correct. For example, answers with words such as *sometimes*, *occasionally*, and even *usually* are typically right.

For example, consider the following question:

Trevor and Joey are college football fans. The following is true about Trevor and Joey:

A. Trevor is a Michigan State fan
B. Joey is a Florida fan
C. Trevor thinks football is better than hockey
D. Joey sometimes cheers for other teams

Because answer D contains the flexible word *sometimes*, it is likely to be the right answer. Now apply the rule to that example. If the question was a maybe because you had eliminated answers A and C, you would then eliminate answer B and correctly guess answer D.

E. The Art of Intelligent Guessing: All of the Above and None of the Above Answers.

If a question contains an answer that is either "All of the above" or "None of the above," you have been given a gift, because these questions can typically be quickly narrowed down to three, two, or one possible correct answers. For example, if a question contains an answer that is "All of the above," then by definition, *all* other answers *must* be correct. So if any of the other answers is not correct, then you can eliminate that answer *and* the "All of the above" response, limiting your possible correct answers to the remaining two.

Likewise, if a question contains an answer that is "None of the above," then, by definition, *none* of the other answers may be correct. First of all, "None of the above" is almost never a correct answer, because that would mean that the test preparer has provided a question and *not* given you the correct answer as one of the options. This is pointless and therefore rarely done, so you can typically eliminate that answer as a possible correct answer. It also typically means that two of the three remaining answers are likely clearly wrong (so as to not make the "none of the above" response a clearly wrong choice), meaning that the correct answer is likely more obvious than with other questions.

F. The Art of Intelligent Guessing: What is the Test Preparer Looking For.

We learned in Chapter 8 that it is important to understand what the test preparer is looking for from the test taker. Examples noted in Chapter 8 are that the National Registry of Emergency Medical Technicians are looking for paramedic examinees to apply basic medical interventions prior to advanced interventions and that the Certified Financial Planning Board is looking for CFP examinees to use conservative investment approaches rather than more risky and aggressive approaches. So when guessing at an answer, ensure that you recognize and apply that principal.

G. The Art of Intelligent Guessing: Questions of Inconsistent Difficulty.

While almost all multiple-choice tests typically consist of a mixture of easy, moderate, and difficult questions, occasionally an examination can be characterized as very easy overall, very difficult overall, very straight forward overall, or very tricky overall. Once you have completed the first several questions of an examination, it should become apparent whether the test is either very difficult or tricky overall. If it is, then you can apply a rule of consistency going forward in responding to questions.

For example, if a test is very difficult or tricky overall, and you suddenly encounter a question that appears to be abnormally straightforward and easy and has one or more very obvious answers, those apparently "obvious" answers are unlikely to be correct, and it is more likely to be nothing more than a trick question. You are therefore better off first carefully rereading the question to identify any aspects you missed during the first read that may have made the question appear too simple. Next, if the question remains simple after the second read, select another answer that is a possible answer and not one of the obvious answers. Trick questions also represent the rare occasion when "none of the above" may, in fact, be the right answer.

For example, let's assume you are taking a test on astronomy that contains a series of very detailed and complex questions and answers and then you suddenly encountered the following question:

The sky is: A. Blue, B. Orange, C. Green, D. None of the above.

Obviously, this appears to be an incredibly simplistic question that is completely inconsistent with the remainder of the exam. Accordingly, the obvious answer, A. Blue, is likely *not* the right answer. In fact, the correct answer is likely D. None of the above with the explanation that the sky is actually not blue but rather simply appears blue from the reflection of the Earth's surface water, which is blue.

Likewise, if a test is very easy or straightforward overall, and you suddenly encounter a question that appears to be abnormally difficult or tricky, then again the apparently obvious answers are unlikely to be correct. This is because the question is likely to be exactly what it appears to be—a trick question.

You should therefore follow the procedure previously described, which is carefully reread the question to identify any aspects you missed during the first read, make sure you understand the question, and confirm whether it is, in fact, tricky or you simply misread it the first time. If your second read clears up the question and makes it consistent with the remainder of the test, then answer the now simple question with the apparent answer. If the question remains difficult or tricky after the second read, select another answer that is a possible answer and not one of the obvious answers. As stated earlier, trick questions also represent the rare occasion when "none of the above" may in fact be the right answer. Another good option with tricky questions is finding the answer that is unlike the others. An example would be as follows:

Which of the following animals would be studied by a herpetologist?

A. Horses
B. Pigs
C. Snakes
D. Cows

Because horses, pigs, and cows are similar in that they are all mammals and farm animals, and a snake is clearly the least consistent answer, *and we assume the test preparer is trying to be difficult or tricky*, the answer likely (and in fact) is C. Snakes.

H. The Art of Intelligent Guessing: Numbers Out of Context.

By definition, finding yourself guessing at a question involving number answers is unlikely. This is because numeric answers typically involve questions containing formulas and math problems rather than concepts that can be more easily narrowed down to two possible correct answers. However, in the event you find yourself with a maybe involving number answers, common sense and logic can typically help you eliminate one of the answers as less likely to be the correct answer.

Going back to the concept that testing is a game, keep in mind that the testing authority wants to win the game by doing everything it can to trick you into selecting the wrong answer. That is why multiple-choice tests will typically use numbers in wrong answers that are similar to the correct answer, either in composition or proximity. That way, if you make a slight miscalculation, you will potentially arrive at the wrong answer.

For example, consider the following question:

The product of 300 × 0.375 equals which of the following:

A. 99.44
B. 157
C. 112.5
D. 114.5

Note that answers C and D are close in proximity to each other, which suggests that one of those two is likely the correct answer. So if you were able to narrow the possible answers to B and C, you would select C, which is the correct answer.

Now consider the next example:

The product of 300 × 0.375 equals which of the following:

A. 94.3
B. 112.5
C. 1.125
D. 189

Note that answers B and C are similar to each other in composition (same individual numbers with the decimal moved two spaces).

Again, if you were able to narrow the possible answers to A and B, you would select B, which is the correct answer.

Also note that in both previous examples, there is one answer that is significantly different than the other three. In the first example it is B. 157, and in the second example it is D. 189. Using the very same logic and reasoning, an answer that is *not* close in composition or proximity to the other answers is not likely to be the correct answer.

Also, if a question involves numbers that are not whole integers or is likely to have an answer that is not a whole integer, you can eliminate any answers that involve whole integers.

For example, consider the following question:

The product of 35.8 × 18 equals which of the following:

A. 687
B. 634.4
C. 841
D. 644.4

Note from the question that the answer is unlikely to be a whole integer, so if you were able to narrow the possible answers to B and D, you would then select your default answer. If your default answer is not one of the two remaining options, you would then apply (in the case of a numbers question) the "very similar but *not* the same answer" concept from subsection C of this Chapter. Applying that concept to the remaining two available answers, since D is numerically closer to the other answers than B, you would select answer D, which is the correct answer.

Another concept of numbers out of context is where possible answers do not match numbers provided in the question. For example, consider the following question:

Susie has four tomatoes, and Kristy has six lemons. Which of the following is true:

A. The girls have five items of fruit
B. The girls have two items of fruit and eight items of vegetables
C. The girls have four items of vegetables and six items of fruit.
D. The girls have ten items of fruit.

Assuming that you did not realize that tomatoes are fruit and not vegetables, you can still eliminate answers A and B, because the numbers are out of context. The question only involves the numbers of 4, 6, and possibly 10 (by adding 4 and 6). So the number 5 (answer A) and the number 2 (answer B) are out of context and wrong. You have effectively reduced the possible answers to C and D. Thereafter, you could next eliminate answer C by applying the concept of the inconsistent difficulty (discussed previously in this chapter), because it appears too obvious and must therefore be a trick question. Hence, you would arrive at the correct answer, which is answer D.

I. The Art of Intelligent Guessing: Narrowing Number Options Without Doing the Math.

Most math questions on multiple-choice tests require the completion of multiple-step formulas. These formulas are often complex and time-consuming. Multiple steps not only lead to needless use of valuable time, but each step also provides an opportunity for a miscalculation and ultimately a wrong answer. Consequently, if you can narrow the possible answers down without the use of the formula, you should do it. The following is an example of a question in which this system would be beneficial:

Kodie, running at a consistent speed from start to finish, can run a marathon in 3 hours, 19 minutes, 25 seconds. Marley, running at a consistent speed from start to finish, can run a marathon in 2 hours, 57 minutes, 41 seconds. If Kodie runs the first half of a marathon, takes a 4 minute and 16 second break, and then has Marley run the second half after that break, how much time, in hours, minutes, and seconds will it take to complete the marathon from start to finish?

A. 2 hours, 59 minutes, 46 seconds
B. 3 hours, 8 minutes, 27 seconds
C. 3 hours, 13 minutes, 11 seconds
D. 3 hours, 15 minutes, 52 seconds

In order to complete this problem using formulas it would require a total of eight steps as follows:

Step 1: convert Kodie's time of 3 hours, 19 minutes, and 25 seconds into the lowest common denominator (seconds) as follows:

3 hours × 60 × 60 = 10,800
19 minutes × 60 = 1,140
10,800 + 1,140 + 25 = 11,965

Step 2: divide Kodie's time in half as follows:

11,965/2 = 5,982.5

Step 3: convert Marley's time of 2 hours, 57 minutes, and 41 seconds into the lowest common denominator (seconds) as follows:

2 hours × 60 × 60 = 7,200
57 × 60 = 3,420
7,200 + 3,420 + 41 = 10,661

Step 4: divide Marley's time in half as follows:

10,661/2 = 5,330.5

Step 5: add the combined half times as follows:

5,982.5 + 5,330.5 = 11,313

Step 6: divide 11,313 by 60 to convert to minutes as follows:

11,313/60 = 188.55

Step 7: divide 188.55 by 60 to convert to hours as follows:

188.55/60 = 3.14 or 3 hours, 8 minutes, 55 seconds

Step 8: add the 4 minute, 16 second break as follows:

55 seconds + 16 seconds = 71 seconds or 1 minute 11 seconds
8 minutes + 4 minutes + 1 minute = 13 minutes
= 3 hours, 13 minutes, 11 seconds

Those eight steps, in addition to eight separate opportunities to make a math error and come up with the wrong answer to the problem, are consuming enough time to cause you to not answer three or four other questions of equal or greater value.

Alternatively, if you simply conclude that an average of Kodie's time of 3 hours, 19 minutes, and 25 seconds (rounding to 3 hours and 20 minutes), and Marley's time of 2 hours, 57 minutes, and 41 seconds (rounding to 2 hours and 58 minutes) is somewhere around 3 hours and 9 minutes plus a 4 minute and 16 second (rounding again to 4 minutes) break, equals approximately 3 hours and 13 minutes. You then find the answer closest to that figure, which is answer C (the correct answer), and move on to the next question.

J. The Art of Logical Guessing: Your Best Guess.

You have learned that guessing should always be done in an intelligent fashion. However, you have also discovered that there are two circumstances in which you must simply "guess". Those are when you encounter a Type II maybe or a default question in which your selected default answer is not an option. In that case, and only in that case, you should simply make your best guess. Two points that must be considered. First, if one of the remaining "best guess" options is A, do not select answer A for the statistical reasons set forth in Chapter 9. Second, do not spend a great deal of time on selecting your best guess. Trust your instincts, select *that* answer, and move to the next question. The reason for the long standing rule of never changing a test answer once you have answered it is simple. Statistically your first instinct is usually correct. So in this case you should "go with your gut" pick your best guess, and move on.

Chapter 11

Scheduling the Exam

As previously stated, the exam should be scheduled based upon the direction of the preparation course you take. Schedule the prep course first and find out from them when they recommend the test be scheduled in relation to completion of the course. Typically, you will want to schedule the test within a few days of completing the course while the study materials are still fresh. However, some preparation courses recommend that a specified period of time elapse before you actually sit for the test, either to complete certain postcourse study or to allow time for the information to settle in.

So, the first step in scheduling your exam is to determine from the testing center how quickly the exam can be scheduled and the test center's policy on cancellation and rescheduling. If the testing center has multiple test site locations to choose from (most do), make sure you review location availability and ensure that the location you desire does not require any additional time prior to scheduling. If, for example, the test center and site you intend to use only require a few days prior notice to schedule, then do not schedule the exam until *after* you complete the exam preparation course. If, in the alternative, the test center requires more than a few days advance notice to schedule, and has a twenty-four—or forty-eight-hour cancellation policy, I recommend you schedule your test a day or two after completion of the preparation course, as you can then cancel the reservation and reschedule if you determine, during the preparation course, you need more time.

If you have the opportunity to schedule different times to take the exam, make sure you schedule the test at a time that works best for you. Because everyone has a different biological clock, determine what time of day you perform best on tests (your peak time), as everyone is different in this regard. Most people do best within an hour or two after waking up in the morning, but everyone is different. Once you have determined your individual peak time, try to schedule the exam at that time of day, giving yourself enough time to get a good night's sleep, get ready (including eating a good meal as described in Chapter 1), have your two-hour last-minute preparation (final review), and still have sufficient time to travel to the test site (doubling the travel time as discussed in Chapter 8). So, for example, if you typically wake up refreshed at 8:00 a.m., need one hour to get ready and eat breakfast, and live thirty minutes away from the test site, you would want to schedule the exam for 12:00 p.m. (eight o'clock to nine o'clock to get ready, nine o'clock to eleven o'clock for final review, and eleven o'clock to twelve o'clock to drive to the exam site).

Chapter 12

The Warm Up: Things to Do Just Prior to Sitting For the Exam

At least twenty-four hours prior to attending the examination, make sure you know exactly what you can and cannot bring to the test site. First, make sure you carefully review the test reservation notification, or if you do not receive one, visit the test site's website or contact the site directly to find out precisely what you can and cannot bring. You do not want to arrive on time to the center and find out you need two pieces of photo ID when you only brought one or that you needed to bring you admission ticket and left it at home. You also want to take the opportunity to determine whether you will have access to scratch paper at the test site while taking the exam (the importance of this will be discussed later).

Second, determine what type of equipment you can bring to the test. If you are allowed to use a calculator during the test, make sure you know what type or models are allowed. Bringing a calculator that you cannot use will not help much. I recommend that if you are allowed to bring and use a calculator, bring two (a primary and a backup), both with fresh batteries. If your calculator breaks or the batteries go dead during the test, that will not help you pass the exam. If you need to bring pencils, make sure you have the right type (typically No. 2) and that they are sharpened and have erasers.

If you wear glasses, make sure you bring a spare set. If you are easily distracted by noise, find out whether you can bring and wear earplugs and, if you are allowed, bring them to the test.

You will also want to bring a watch so that you will be able to monitor your time during the test. If you are taking a paper test (as opposed to a test on a computer), you will also want to bring at least two highlighters (which will be discussed further in Chapter 7).

Once you have identified everything you can and will bring, make up a checklist of those items. This should be done several days before the scheduled exam. You should gather all of these items the day before the exam, go over each item with your checklist, and place them, along with the checklist, in a secure spot.

The evening before the test, place all of the items and your checklist in the passenger seat of the vehicle you will be driving to the test site. The next morning, before your leave, make sure everything from your checklist is, in fact, there. Regardless of whether you are allowed to bring food to the test site, bring a bottle of water and a small snack, like a power bar or a package of peanut butter crackers (something that will provide some quick energy) in case you get a break during the test.

The day before the exam (relax day) should be a day to allow your mind and body to relax and refresh. If you have followed the schedule you developed as discussed in Chapter 4, you should be at a point where the preparation course has been completed, all postcourse study requirements have been completed, you have completed the highlight and line out process described in Chapter 5, and you have memorized the memory hooks and formulas in Chapter 6. In sum, you are intellectually prepared for the test.

On relax day, you should do exactly that—relax. If you work at a job that involves stress or mental challenges, take this day off. Get a good night's sleep the night before relax day and set your alarm to get up at the same time you will be getting up on test day. This will establish your biological clock on schedule and ensure your sleep is on schedule and uninterrupted the night before the exam. Make sure you eat properly during relax day.

Stay away from spicy, fatty, or other foods that may upset you digestive system, which might interfere with your sleep that night or your ability to concentrate on the exam the next day.

At some point during the day, you should also figure out how much time you will need to do a final review of any remaining highlight items still not fully absorbed from your study materials or notes, as well as a review of your cheat sheet, including all memory hooks and formulas (final review). If that is, for example, two hours, then go through those notes, formulas, and memory hooks once just prior to going to sleep. That final review study session should be the *only* time you study during relax day.

You should also do a trial run on the travel to the test site. If the test site is within one hour of your residence, drive to the test site, preferably at the same time of day you will be traveling on test day. That way, you will make sure you know exactly where you are going (including the exact location and available parking) and exactly how much drive time you will have (with similar traffic patterns). You will also be able to confirm whether your directions are correct and whether construction or other travel impediments exist and how to best avoid them. Getting lost or stuck in traffic is not a good way to begin test day.

The morning of the exam, you want to dress with at least one additional layer of clothing (such as a sweater or sweatshirt) over warm weather clothing (such as a T-shirt or other short-sleeved shirt). Regardless of the temperature outside, test sites are typically air conditioned and are often not properly temperature controlled. In other words, you want to dress appropriately for a test site that may be anywhere from 60°F to 80°F and be dressed for comfort for either extreme.

Eat a good meal (as described in Chapter 1). Resist the urge to drink energy drinks or excess coffee as the "crash" later will negatively affect your ability to pass the exam.

The morning of the exam, you want to complete a second final review. This should be done after you get *ready* and *before* you travel to the test site. *Do not do your final review while driving to the test site.* It is difficult to do well on a test from the back of a police car or ambulance. Double-check to make sure you have all the items from your checklist, including any admission ticket and photo ID required to be provided at check-in. Depart for the test site, giving yourself at least two times the actual drive time with a minimum of thirty minutes extra time (so if it is thirty minutes, leave one hour before hand, etc.).

Upon arrival at the test site (and while still inside your vehicle in the parking area), take a few minutes to once again go over your cheat sheet. The primary reason to do this is so you can immediately write down your memory hooks and formulas on any available scratch paper you will have access to during the test.

Chapter 13

Post Check-In/Pretest Activities

Once you have checked into the test site, find out from the staff whether you can leave your seat once seated. If you cannot, then the first thing to do is orient yourself to the facility *before* you are seated. You should start by going to the nearest restroom, not only to use it prior to the exam but also to know exactly where it is in the event you have to go again during the test. Since the clock rarely stops during a bathroom break, you do not want to waste valuable test time wandering the halls looking for a restroom.

Once you are to be seated, unless seats are preassigned, take the time to select a good seat. A good seat is one that is not under a heat or air conditioning duct and isn't close to any doors or the check-in area where activity during the test may be distracting. A good seat is also not at the back of the room where hearing pretest directions and time notifications may be difficult. Beyond that, select a seat that will best ensure your comfort during the exam.

Once seated for the exam, but before the exam starts, you want to immediately write down all of your memory hooks on the scratch paper so you will have access to them during the exam. You also want to take the time to set up your area, placing your equipment, pencils, and clock or watch in positions convenient to you during the exam.

Typically, there will be instructions for the test, provided either orally by the staff or in writing in the form of a handout, test cover sheet, or computer screen. Make sure you pay attention and fully understand all instructions, especially those relating to time limits and question values. Frequently, tests have certain sections that have higher point values than others. This is very important information and will be discussed in detail later. Another piece of critically important information, if your test is computer-based, is whether you have the ability to skip questions you are uncertain about and return to them later and if you are able to change answers.

Now that you are about to begin the exam, here is the single most important point in this entire book. Just before you open the test book or click the "begin the test" button on the computer, take a deep breath, take a minute to stretch, and remind yourself of two inalienable truths. First, you have done everything you need to do to fully and properly prepare for the exam, and you *are* ready. Second, there is no reason to worry, because you will either do well or you won't, and on the off chance you do not do well, you can always simply retest and improve your score. So don't worry. Just attack!

Chapter 14

Taking the Retest

Hopefully this book will allow you to pass your test the first time and avoid having to retake the test. However, in the event you are now preparing for a retest, the following are some additional recommendations.

Your first task is to determine why you failed the test the first time. Sometimes the answer is obvious. If you were grossly unprepared due to lack of prestudy or failed to manage your time correctly during the exam and had to guess the last half of the test because time expired, then you presumably know what you did wrong. Therefore, you also know what you now have to do to pass the second time around. However, most second-time test takers lack a clear understanding of what they did wrong or why they failed. In fact, many individuals who scored poorly on their first attempt frequently believe they did well prior to receiving their scores. If you fit into this latter category, it is critical that you find out precisely why you failed the first time, so you can complete a focused program of improvement prior to the retest.

Some testing authorities will provide you with written feedback along with your overall score, clearly noting which areas caused you difficulty. Others will provide that information on request. In the event you have feedback, carefully review the areas in which you performed poorly. However, before you simply restudy the areas and topics you had difficulty with, first review the areas you did well on and contemplate what it was about your study methods or that topic that caused you to do well. Then take those same methodologies and apply them to your restudy of the areas in which you did not perform well.

Retaking the prep course is another option. You should consult with the providers of the prep course you took initially to obtain their thoughts on this option. Most reputable test preparation courses will not recommend that you retake their course unless it is truly likely to help you pass the second time.

Chapter 15

Sample Test Questions

Now that you understand the systems required to master the multiple-choice test, we can now apply those principles to actual multiple-choice questions. Let's begin by using several questions to prove the concept of the default answer. I want to begin here, because it is just as important that you truly believe in the systems you have been taught in this book as it is you understand them. So we begin by applying and proving the concept of the default answer. If you have not already selected your default answer, select one now (B, C, or D) for purposes of the following sample test. Next, answer each of the following intentionally difficult questions by responding with your best guess (*not* your default answer), marking the questions you know the answer to. Then check your answers against the answer key provided and note you score.

When you are finished, go back and retake the test, but this time, answer each question you originally guessed at with your selected default answer. Then check your revised answers against the key and see how many questions you answered correctly using the default answer system. I think you will find you did much better the second time with default answers. Go ahead and begin:

1. Which state has the most National Parks at five?

   A. Arizona
   B. California
   C. Utah
   D. Washington

2. Who was the pope in 467 A.D.?

   A. St. Felix
   B. St. Hilarius
   C. St. Leo
   D. St. Marcus

3. Dysprosium is which numbered element on the periodic chart?

   A. 43
   B. 66
   C. 84
   D. 107

4. Which amendment to the U.S. Constitution banned poll tax in federal elections?

   A. XVI
   B. XIV
   C. XXIV
   D. XXVII

5. Which of the following snakes is responsible for the most human deaths each year?

   A. Black mamba
   B. Anaconda
   C. Tiger snake
   D. Carpet viper

6. Which of the following countries hosted the most modern Olympic Games as of 1992?

   A. France
   B. Germany
   C. Greece
   D. Japan

7. Which of the following individuals performed in the most Hollywood film productions?

   A. John Wayne
   B. Gene Hackman
   C. Lon Chaney
   D. Mel Blanc

8. The average Ph level for sea water is which of the following?

   A. 7.2
   B. 7.4
   C. 7.8
   D. 8.0

9. Which of the following states was admitted to the Union on May 29, 1848?

   A. California
   B. Kansas
   C. Oregon
   D. Wisconsin

10. Which of the following artists has had the most Top 10 singles, dead or alive?

   A. Elvis Presley
   B. Madonna
   C. The Beatles
   D. Michael Jackson

11. In 1995, the most common religion in Europe and Asia was which of the following?

   A. Buddhism
   B. Christianity
   C. Hinduism
   D. Islam

12. Which of the following sharks is responsible for the most human deaths each year?

   A. Bull shark
   B. Great white shark
   C. Hammerhead shark
   D. Tiger shark

13. The film *Napoleon Dynamite* was filmed in which State?

   A. Utah
   B. Kansas
   C. Idaho
   D. Colorado

14. Which of the following languages is most commonly spoken on the African continent?

   A. Berber
   B. Swahili
   C. Arabic
   D. French

15. Which of the following mathematicians is credited for the development of differential and integral calculus?

   A. Archimedes
   B. Pierre De Fermat
   C. Albert Einstein
   D. Isaac Newton

16. Sarah Childress is the maiden name of the wife of which of the following U.S. presidents?

   A. Franklin Pierce
   B. James Polk
   C. Zachary Taylor
   D. John Tyler

17. The third wealthiest man in the world, after Bill Gates and Warren Buffet, lives in which of the following countries?

   A. Germany
   B. Saudi Arabia
   C. Sweden
   D. Mexico

18. In 2007, on which of the following continents were the most new automobiles purchased?

   A. Africa
   B. Asia
   C. Europe
   D. North America

19. Which of the following artists painted the most expensive painting ever sold at private auction?

   A. Jackson Pollack
   B. Pablo Picasso
   C. Michael Angelo
   D. Vincent Van Gogh

20. The terrain of China is made up principally of which of the following?

    A. Deciduous forests and grassy plains
    B. Tundra and coniferous forests
    C. Tropical rain forests and rice patty marshes
    D. Desert and mountains

21. Which Arkansas wildflower grows from April through May?

    A. Black-eyed susan
    B. Indian paintbrush
    C. Bird's foot violet
    D. Mexican hat

22. How many inventions did Thomas Edison hold patents on?

    A. 37
    B. 146
    C. 258
    D. 1,093

23. What is the third most common religion among natives of Hawaii?

    A. Buddhism
    B. Judaism
    C. Hinduism
    D. Confucianism

24. As of 2009, which college team held the most NCAA Division I championships?

    A. University of Iowa
    B. Oklahoma State
    C. University of Minnesota
    D. Iowa State

25. U.S. Presidents Martin Van Buren (1836) and Millard Fillmore (1850) were born in which of the following states?

    A. Virginia
    B. Ohio
    C. New York
    D. Massachusetts

26. The average annual temperature (in degrees Fahrenheit) in Annette, Alaska is:

    A. 16 degrees
    B. 26 degrees
    C. 36 degrees
    D. 46 degrees

27. Who was the last National Hockey League player to score at least fifty goals in the first fifty games of a season?

    A. Brett Hull
    B. Wayne Gretski
    C. Mario Lemieux
    D. Alexander Moqilny

28. As of 2002, which bear has killed more humans in North America than any other?

    A. Grizzly bear
    B. Kodiak bear
    C. Black bear
    D. Brown bear

29. The founder of the Buddhist religion was which of the following?

    A. Shakyamuni Krishna
    B. Siddhartha Gautama
    C. Gotama Buddha
    D. Ghamahsi Vishnu

30. The Azores Islands were discovered by which famous explorer:

    A. Christopher Columbus
    B. Marco Polo
    C. Ferdinand Magellan
    D. Prince Henry

31. Which of the following candidates has appeared on the ballot in the most U.S. presidential elections since 1900?

    A. Franklin Roosevelt (Democrat)
    B. Earl Dodge (Prohibition)
    C. Richard Nixon (Republican)
    D. Ralph Nader (Independent)

32. The largest galaxy in the universe is which of the following?

    A. IC1011 galaxy
    B. Milky Way galaxy
    C. Abell 2029 galaxy
    D. Elliptical galaxy

Check your answers against the answer key on the next page.

Answer Key

1. C
2. B
3. B
4. C
5. D
6. A
7. D
8. C
9. D
10. B
11. B
12. A
13. C
14. C
15. D
16. B
17. D
18. C
19. A
20. D
21. C
22. D
23. B
24. B
25. C
26. D
27. A
28. C
29. B
30. D
31. B
32. A

Next we will apply other concepts learned in this book to actual test questions in order to maximize the likelihood of success in mastering the multiple-choice exam. We will begin with a multiple-option question (discussed in Chapter 8):

Trevor is an estate planning attorney with no other professional designations. When clients ask him for help with investments and retirement planning, he reviews their investment portfolio and financial situation. He typically charges his hourly rate for these financial services and often recommends mutual funds and bank certificates of deposit as investment tools. Which of the following applies to Trevor:

1. Trevor is a certified financial planner.
2. Trevor is compensated for financial advice.
3. Trevor is an investment advisor and fiduciary.
4. Trevor should be securities licensed.
5. Trevor may be subject to criminal penalties.

A. 1, 2, and 4
B. 2, 3, 4, and 5
C. All apply
D. None apply

Now let's go through the proper steps of attacking this question.

Step one: Read the question.

Step two: Read statement 1 and compare it to the question. If it is incorrect, line it out and then also line out every answer that indicates statement 1 is correct.

In the case of this particular question, if you were studying for the CFP exam, you would know statement 1 is incorrect, so you would then line out and eliminate answers A and C.

Step three: Read statement 2 and compare it to the question. If it is incorrect, line it out and then also line out every answer that indicates statement 2 is correct. If statement 2 is correct, then line out every other answer that does not contain statement 2 as an option.

In the case of this particular question, Trevor *is* being compensated for investment advice (even though he is not properly licensed to do so), so statement 2 is correct. Accordingly, you would line out answer D, leaving answer B as the only possible (and, in fact) correct answer.

Next let's look at a question that involves an "all of the above" or "none of the above" answer (discussed in Chapter 10):

Which of the following are traits typically found in women as financial planning clients?

A. Women are more likely than men to ask for advice.
B. Women are much more likely to take risks when investing money.
C. Unlike men, women rarely set goals.
D. All of the above.

If we had studied properly for this exam, we would know that answer A is true. Had Answer D been "none of the above," we could have eliminated that answer through answer A being correct. However, because answer A is true, answers A and D are still viable answers. Next, we look at answer B, and because we know answer B is false, we can then eliminate answers B and D and, presumably, answer C. However, we should read answer C to make sure that is also not a correct answer. Upon reading answer C, we realize that is also false, so we mark answer A as the correct answer (and a given and therefore *not* marked for review) and move on to the next question.

Now let's review a question that has two similar answers and numbers out of context (discussed Chapter 10):

Kristyisaparamedictransportingapregnanttwenty-two-year-old female patient from a small medical clinic to the nearest hospital. The doctor at the clinic informs Kristy that the patient is gravida 3 and parity 2. That information tells Kristy:

A. The patient has given birth 2 times and has had 1 abortion.
B. The patient has given birth 2 times and has had no abortions.
C. The patient has given birth 3 times with only 2 surviving children.
D. The patient has 3 children delivered and has had 3 miscarriages.

Let's assume we know that gravida is number of pregnancies but are unsure what parity is. We would begin by eliminating all answers that do not indicate three pregnancies, which would be answers B and D. Having narrowed down the correct answers to answer A or answer C, using the rule of similar answers, you would see that answers A and B are very similar. Because B has been eliminated, you would answer A, which is the correct answer.

But let's assume instead you did not know what gravida meant but understood parity to mean number of live baby deliveries. We would begin by eliminating all answers that do not indicate two live births, which would be answers C and D. Then, applying the concept of inconsistent numbers, since the question has the numbers three and two, answer B is also incorrect as it has only the number two and no other number that would account for the number three in the question. Thus, you have eliminated all other answers other than answer A, which is correct.

Let's next look at a question that involves both an extent and limitation question (discussed in Chapter 7) and what the test preparer is looking for (discussed in Chapters 5 and 10):

Susie, who is a paramedic, has a twenty-eight-year-old female patient who is unconscious, not breathing, and pulseless. The first course of action for Susie would be which of the following?

A. Administer 1mg of epinephrine IV push.
B. Clear the airway and begin CPR.
C. Defibrillate at 200 joules.
D. If the airway is not patent, intubate and begin positive pressure ventilations.

First you should note from the question the extent and limitation word of first, so the questions is *not* asking what is the correct procedure. It is asking what the *first* correct procedure is. Because all of these answers are technically correct, failure to note that qualifier would be disastrous. Next we apply the concept of what the test preparer is looking for. Because National Registry wants paramedics to provide basic interventions first, we can eliminate answers A, C, and D, because all three involve advanced procedures, leaving the basic procedure and correct answer, which is answer B.

Let's next look at a standardized aptitude test question (in this case, the LSAT) involving a multiple-option question in which the answer is actually given to you by the facts of the question, but answering the question quickly is paramount:

Susie, Katie, and Ronnie are bus drivers that make one trip each day, and they are the only ones that take riders 1, 2, 3, 4, 5, 6, and 7. The following are additional facts about the buses and riders:

1. Neither 5 nor 7 take Susie's bus on a day when 2 takes Susie's bus.
2. 7 does not take Katie's bus on a day when 2 does.
3. When 1 and 6 take the same bus, it is always Ronnie's bus
4. 3 always takes Ronnie's bus.

Given the foregoing facts, which of the same buses could 2, 3, and 7 could take on a given day.

A. Susie only
B. Katie only
C. Ronnie only
D. Katie and Ronnie only
E. Susie, Katie, and Ronnie

We would begin by noting that the only relevant riders are 2, 3, and 7. Looking then at fact 1, we see that 2 and 7 cannot ride Susie's bus together, so answers A and E are lined out. We then look at fact 2 and see that 2 and 7 cannot ride Katie's bus, so we can next line out answers B and D. We need to go no further, as answer C is the only remaining (and correct) answer.

Let's look at a question involving an absolute and the same answer (discussed in Chapter 10):

How many persons covered under federal disability programs have no need for additional disability income?

A. All
B. Most
C. Some
D. A few

We can begin by eliminating answer A, as all is an absolute answer and therefore extremely unlikely to be correct. We can next eliminate answers C and D, because some and a few are essentially the same answer, leaving B. Most as the correct response.

Another example of a similar question would be as follows:

Social Security Disability pays _____ income to supply total disability coverage for persons earning minimum wage.

A. Sufficient
B. Insufficient
C. Generally insufficient
D. Nonexistent

Once again, we can begin by eliminating answer D, as nonexistent is an absolute answer and therefore extremely unlikely to be correct. We can next eliminate answers B and C, because insufficient and generally insufficient are essentially the same answer, leaving A. Sufficient as the correct response.

The next question is an example of narrowing the number option without doing the math (as described in Chapter 10), as well as a too much time question (as described in Chapter 5):

If Joey can paint a house in 4 hours, and Trevor can paint the same house in 6 hours, how long will it take for both Joey and Trevor to paint the house together?

A. 2 hours, 24 minutes
B. 3 hours, 12 minutes
C. 4 hours, 10 minutes
D. 4 hours, 33 minutes

Again, you can spend the time required to go through the precise exercise of calculating the applicable formulas to arrive at the exact answer, hoping you do not make any math errors along the way. However, you are much better off simply noting that Joey can paint half the house in about two hours and Trevor in about three, so the answer is somewhere between two and three hours. Because answer A is the only answer that fits that requirement, pick (the correct) answer A and go on to the next question.

Finally, let's work through the exercise of givens, maybes, and defaults (as described in Chapters 7, 8, 9 and 10). The first example involves a standardized test which allows questions to be marked for review. We will use the same question for all seven possible scenarios as follows:

Gerald M. Morello Jr. is which of the following:

A. Attorney at Law
B. Financial Advisor
C. Electrician
D. Stand up Comic

The correct answer is Answer A. So, for example, if you knew the correct answer was answer A, it would be a given, you would mark answer A, *not* mark the question for review, and go to the next question.

If you were somewhat confident that the answer was A but not completely sure, it would be a Type I maybe, so you would mark answer A, *not* mark the question for review, and go to the next question. If you were unsure of the answer but could eliminate with certainty all but two of the possible answers (let's say answers C and D, and were therefore left with only A or B as possible alternatives), it would be a Type II maybe. You would then go through the process of intelligently guessing the correct answer on a Type II maybe as set forth in Chapter 8. If that process leads you to the correct answer, mark that answer, do *not* mark the question for review, and go to the next question.

If the previous Type II maybe scenario is present and intelligent guessing does not lead you to an answer, then mark your default answer, mark the question for review, and go to the next question. When returning to this question later, you would *only* change the answer if the requirements set forth in Chapter 8 on changing answers are met.

If the previous Type II maybe scenario is present and, after completing the process of intelligent guessing, one of the remaining two options is *not* your default answer, then mark the question for review and go to the next question. When returning to this question later, if the question is now a given mark that answer. Otherwise, select your "best guess" between the two optional answers, avoiding answer A for the statistical reasons discussed previously, and go to the next question.

If you are unsure of the correct answer and cannot narrow the options down to two, simply mark the default answer, mark the question for review, and go to the next question. When returning to this question later you would *only* change the answer if the requirements set forth in Chapter 8 on changing answers are met, then go to the next question.

If you are unsure of the correct answer and cannot narrow the options down to two, but can absolutely eliminate the default answer, and *only* the default answer, leaving three others, leave the question unanswered, mark the question for review, and go to the next question. When returning to this question later, go through the process of intelligent guessing. If that process does not lead you to an answer, then select your best guess, avoiding answer A for the statistical reasons discussed previously, and go to the next question.

Now let's work through that same exercise of givens, maybes, and defaults with a standardized test that does not allow questions to be marked for review. We will use the same question for all seven possible scenarios as follows:

Barbra Losi has several pets. Her two dogs are named:

A. Milo and Jada
B. Kodie and Eddie
C. Bowser and Happy
D. Kobe and Marley

The correct answer is Answer A. So, for example, if you knew the correct answer was answer A, it would be a given, you would mark answer A and go to the next question.

If you were somewhat confident that the answer was A but not completely sure, it would be a Type I maybe, so you would mark answer A and go to the next question.

If you were unsure of the answer but could eliminate with certainty all but two of the possible answers (let's say answers C and D, and were therefore left with only A or B as possible alternatives), it would be a Type II maybe. You would then go through the process of intelligently guessing the correct answer on a Type II maybe as set forth in Chapter 8, mark that answer and go to the next question.

If the previous Type II maybe scenario is present and intelligent guessing does not lead you to an answer, then mark your default answer, and go to the next question.

If the previous Type II maybe scenario is present and, after completing the process of intelligent guessing, one of the remaining two options is *not* your default answer, then make your "best guess" between the two optional answers, avoiding answer A for the statistical reasons discussed previously, and go to the next question.

If you are unsure of the correct answer and cannot narrow the options down to two, simply mark the default answer, and go to the next question.

If you are unsure of the correct answer and cannot narrow the options down to two, but can absolutely eliminate the default answer, and *only* the default answer, leaving three others, go through the process of intelligent guessing. If that process does not lead you to an answer, then select your best guess, avoiding answer A for the statistical reasons discussed previously, and go to the next question.

Chapter 16

Conclusion

You are now equipped with all of the requisite knowledge, ability, and wherewithal to attack and conquer any and all multiple-choice examinations. If you put in the time and effort to properly prepare pursuant to the methods outlined in this book and have the discipline and focus to implement the systems you have been taught, you will maximize your performance and achieve superlative results. Do not lose sight of the fact that multiple-choice testing is nothing more than a game. You can and will win if you play by my rules. Good luck and good hunting.

CPSIA information can be obtained at www.ICGtesting.com
Printed in the USA
LVOW05s0715040913

350858LV00001B/77/P